Katobole Folklore And Livingstone's Epic Journey

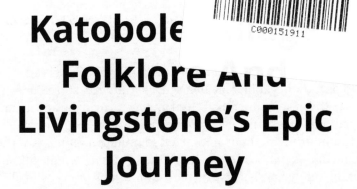
Untold stories of the 1873 Epic Journey

Unrewarded heroism of Livingstone's African porters

By
CHENGO MULALA

KATOBOLE VILLAGE FOLKLORE AND LIVINGSTONE'S EPIC JOURNEY

Publisher
Chengo Mulala Publishing
www.chengomulalapublishing.com

First Edition
ISBN-13: 978-1-8384418-0-7 - E-book
ISBN-13: 978-1-8384418-1-4 - Paperback

Printed in the
United Kingdom and United States of America

Publishing Consultants
Vike Springs Publishing Ltd.
www.vikesprings.com

For Bookings and Speaking Engagements, Contact Us:
Grace - Email: gracechamapupe@gmail.com
Grace's books are available at special discounts when purchased in bulk for promotions or as donations for educational and training purposes.

Limit of Liability/Disclaimer of Warranty

This publication is designed to provide accurate and authoritative information in regard to the subject matter covered. It is sold with the understanding that the publisher and author are not engaged in rendering physiological advice, and the author makes no representations or warranties with respect to the completeness of the contents of this work. Neither the publisher nor the author shall be liable for damages arising here from. The fact that an organisation or website is referred to in this work as a citation and/or a potential source of further information does not mean that the author or the publisher endorses the information that the organisation or website may provide, or recommendations it may make. Due to the ever-changing information from the web, Internet websites and URLs listed in this work may have changed or been removed.

All trademarks or names referenced in this book are the property of their respective owners, and the publisher and author are not associated with any product or vendor mentioned.

DEDICATION

This book is written in memory of my charismatic, cunning and brave maternal grandfather, Ngosa Kabaso Shompolo Mulutula. Without his part in the story of Scottish missionary and explorer Dr David Livingstone, Katobole village, where I grew up in Africa, would never have been established.

Grandad might not have known that he was to be part of an iconic chapter of 19th century colonial history, nor did he know that one free-spirited granddaughter would, after many years, bring to light historical events and the hilarious stories told by him, at Katobole village.

If he could look down and see me now, he would be beyond belief to find he was the source of a dynastic family whose offspring would achieve even greater things and keep Katobole village glowing in the dark continent of Africa, and immortalising Mulutula as one of the 19th century Zambian icons.

I also give credit to Dr David Livingstone himself. If not for him, my Grandad Mulutula would not have married into royalty and produced the line that resulted in the large family of which I am a part.

This book is also dedicated to my late father Mr Jairous Katebe Chama, who pushed me beyond my wildest educational and professional dreams. Other emotional thanks go to my late brother Mr John Jairous Chama who stood in to be my saviour in the absence of my father. For example, when Dad was hospitalised in Zaire, and again when Dad was imprisoned for his political stance against colonial rule. Incidentally, when my teenage brother could not afford fares for me to go to my boarding school (60-70 miles from our village) he picked up his bicycle and we waded through wild African rivers to ensure I got to school.

Lastly, I would like to dedicate this book to my ancestor Princess Chengo Mulala, whose teenage courage and tenacity turned her life from rags to riches. And to my grandmother Lucia Mulala and my mother Besa Milika Mulutula who instilled in me a sense of self-belief, liberal thinking, humanity, tenacity and a strong will to survive. I salute you all!!

ACKNOWLEDGEMENTS

This piece of work would not be complete without giving credit to many dedicated people who worked and contributed tirelessly to ensure the book was written in the most professional, impartial and respectful manner.

At a time when I despaired of ever finding an editor for my book, by chance I attended The Winning Women Essex event in Southend-on-Sea where I met Janice Gilbert of WordPerfectProof. Through editing my book, she took it on like her own story. She loved the African village tales and actually led me towards a more focused and professional way of telling my childhood stories.

Many thanks go to my baby sister Rhoidah Kyanamina who shared with me her own memories of Grandad's eccentric stories. Over many late-night telephone conversations, we would often be in tears of laughter remembering the things Grandad said or did.

I'm grateful to my Uncle Peter Mulutula Ngelesani who, at 93 years old, was the oldest of Grandad Mulutula's surviving blood relatives.

Uncle Peter helped me with the authenticity of the stories of Katobole village and issues related to inheritance tradition. Unfortunately, Uncle Peter Ngelesani and his son Peter (Junior) passed away before the book was published.

To friends who have contributed to this project in so many ways, too many to mention individually (nonetheless you know who you are), I can only say thank you very, very much.

To my family who have stood solidly behind me with my ever-changing plans. You have been there when I needed you most. You are my biggest critics but most of all, you have accepted me, as your mother, the risk-taker, the free-spirited, creative person. I truly care about you all – and whatever I do, I do it for you! Thank you, my darlings!

To my spiritual and inspirational guru, Mwata, who picked up my broken pieces and made me feel whole once again. You are my pillar, my love and my soulmate. You have brought stability, calmness and joy to my life. You are the air I breathe. Since the day we met, you have engulfed me in a bubble of spiritual peace and calmness. You have given me a shoulder to cry on. I truly appreciate your loving and calming influence.

TABLE OF CONTENTS

INTRODUCTION

What made me write this book about Dr David Livingstone?

An unexpected phone call came from a Scottish lady who introduced herself as Jo Vallis. She said she had read something about the book I had written on dementia awareness in Zambia. She said she was very excited to read a book written by a British/Zambian author and that she had decided to give me a call. She then told me that she was born in Zambia of Scottish parentage. Her grandfather was one of the Scottish missionaries who were sent to Malawi in Africa to complete Dr Livingstone's legacy of building and spreading Christianity in Southern African countries.

During our telephone conversation, I told Jo Vallis about my family's connections with the final journey of Dr David Livingstone's embalmed body from Chitambo where he had died, to Dar-es-Salaam in East Africa for shipment to the United Kingdom across the Indian Ocean and the Mediterranean Sea. Jo was interested in my story and encouraged me to write a book about it.

However, what I did not remember at the time was that I had already started writing Grandad's stories which I sometimes read to my children when they were young. We could spend the whole afternoon arguing about Grandad's stories. Then I would detect some vibes of jealousy from their father who would deliberately join the group and start telling the children fictitious stories of how he had crossed a river full of crocodiles or how he was chased by a lion. The children would obviously change sides and start cheering and laughing at whatever stories he invented there and then. To avoid any friction or disagreement, I would quietly gather my papers and sit in another room where I typed the stories and saved them onto a USB and which, through frustration, I hid in cupboard drawers and literally forgot about.

But after talking to Jo, I decided to look for the saved drafts. When I found the USB, I could not believe the richness and authenticity of the material I had written such a long time ago. I therefore made up my mind to take on the project of writing a book about my grandfather's involvement in Dr David Livingstone's epic journey of 1873.

Writing this book makes me feel content and proud of my ancestors of whom I have written and whose stories will be read by many people. I feel as though I am opening the doors to my family home. I sometimes get compliments from genuine people who wish they could write stories about their ancestors as well. At the same time, I also get negative feedback or reviews which I recognise as sour grapes. These are friends or people I barely know who say things like "I am going to write a sensational novel or spy story which will be better than your book." I just take their comments as water off a duck's back and say things like, "That's good," and wish them the best of luck!

Coming back to Dr David Livingstone, much has been written about his epic last journey but the African porters have barely been mentioned, even though Dr Livingstone himself had so much compassion for them.

Unlike Marco Polo and his Asian expeditions, Livingstone did not have an army of soldiers marching with him through the thick African forests and crocodile-infested rivers during his 19th century expeditions. He depended on the hospitality he received from his African hosts, whom he respected and treated more or less like equals (unlike the views held by European explorers at the time). Livingstone maintained that the African social habits and attitudes had a purpose and he sometimes felt that Africans were harmed, rather than helped, by European colonial attitudes and influence.

Dr David Livingstone was born at Blantyre, Lanarkshire, near Glasgow in Scotland on 19th March 1813, and died on 4th May 1873 at Chitambo's Village, Serenje District, Zambia. Dr Livingstone had been trained as a missionary doctor. However, after turning down missionary jobs in the West

Indies and China, he eventually arrived at Cape Town, South Africa in 1840.

After observing missionary work being carried out around Cape Town and Kuruman, Livingstone grew weary and disillusioned with traditional missioning and was surprised to discover that only forty converts had been achieved in twenty years of missionary labour, and that those missionaries and mission societies had to exaggerate the number of converts in order to keep funds flowing from sponsors in the UK. He became bored, and wrote to his family in England that there was little for him to do at Kuruman and that "inactivity was anathema to his autodidact". In a disillusioned state of mind, young Dr Livingstone wrote:

"There is a lamentable deadness prevailing in the whole of this field – there are no conversions, the only work proceeding with anything like briskness is Moffat's translation of the Bible into the language of the people."

Dr Livingstone then started undertaking journeys northward with other explorers, and the most talked about wealthy Englishman, William Cotton, who started sponsoring Livingstone's journeys to the south-west border of Zimbabwe. He enjoyed the companionship of his Tswana servants whose customs, language and way of thinking he could tolerate and reckon with. It has been suggested that perhaps because Livingstone was Scottish, he felt alienated from the English, hence Livingstone respected his African companions and treated them, if not as equals, at least as worthy of tolerance and understanding.

Susi and Chuma

In 1861, Livingstone rescued two eleven-year-old boys, Chuma and Wekotani, from a slave trader by sawing off their slave chains with his own hands. On 10th December 1865, the two boys were baptised in the presence of Livingstone as John Wekotani and James Chuma. However, Dr Livingstone was happy to release his third African servant Wekotani when he showed interest in getting married and returning to his people. Most accounts tell us that Susi and Chuma had been Livingstone's longest standing servants and remained faithful to him up to the end, but it was important to Livingstone that the boys remained servants and never behaved as slaves to him.

Livingstone's Recruitment in India 1865

Whilst making preparations for his 1865 expedition, on his return trip from England and while he was in India, Livingstone ignored the inclusion of fellow whites in his expedition and instead picked up the two boys, Susi and Chuma, whom he had left in India after finding them jobs before he left for Great Britain in 1862.

Livingstone recruited about thirty young men and boys to support him on this expedition, including Jacob Wainwright (a Yao boy rescued from slave traders and later sent to the Nassik School in India to learn English). Jacob became the only literate African servant and was also the only chosen African servant to escort Dr David Livingstone's coffin to Great Britain in 1873.

When Livingstone succumbed to fatal illness and was unable to walk, his African servants carried him in a hammock and nursed him all the way until they reached Chitambo's Village on the Bangweulu Swamps where he died on 4th May 1873.

New Recruits to Livingstone's Entourage (the Great Epic Journey)

On the way to East Africa, the entourage carrying Dr Livingstone's remains continued recruiting porters as they trekked many miles through the African forests and villages. One of the new recruits was a village teenager, known as Kabaso Ngosa Mulutula, my maternal grandfather.

Mulutula's father's village was situated along Lake Bangweulu plains along the route used by Livingstone's entourage. The choice of Mulutula was inevitable because of his popularity in the area as a fierce young boxer. No doubt the senior porters were eager to reinforce the group with strong and able-bodied young men who could carry out the task and fight off any hostile villagers on the way.

Faithful to the End

With the African porters' unbelievable defiance, determination, tenacity and bravery, Dr Livingstone's embalmed body was safely delivered to the British Authorities in East Africa, even though the seventy-nine African porters dismissed afterwards have never been mentioned nor compensated for their part in the Epic Journey.

CHAPTER ONE

DR DAVID LIVINGSTONE
THE ABOLITIONIST

This story begins at the end of someone's life. The British missionary and explorer Dr David Livingstone, whom we have read about in our history lessons, was an optimistic idealist who achieved his aim of opening a way into Africa for others, and played a huge part in the eventual abolition of the slave trade that was rife in Africa in the Victorian years. He played an equally important part in the author's ancestry.

If you have never visited Victoria Falls, it is something you really should add to your to-do list. The wonder it inspired in Livingstone, who was the first Western man to discover the falls deep in the forests of Africa, is still a pleasure to read:

"The snow-white sheet seemed like myriads of small comets all rushing in one direction, each of which left behind its nucleus rays of foam... It had never before been seen by European eyes, but scenes so lovely must have been gazed upon by angels in their flight."

The town which grew up on the edge of the falls still bears the name of Livingstone in his memory.

Livingstone's intention was to be a missionary in Africa but he was enchanted by this wonderful continent and led many expeditions into the unexplored territories. He began to prefer to hire Africans to accompany him on these journeys; he would recruit freed African slaves and apparently even rescued two eleven-year-old boys (one of them named James Chuma) from a slave trader by sawing off their slave chains with his own hands. But it was important to Livingstone that these men and boys remained servants and never behaved as slaves to him.

He developed such empathy and rapport with the Africans that he even found jobs for them in India when he had to return to England in 1862. And when ill health and finally his death prevented him progressing any further, the native Africans, among whom he had lived and worked for so many years, were loyal to the end. They carefully embalmed his body and prepared it for the long journey to the east coast of Africa, where it would be transported to his people in Great Britain.

Livingstone's companions and servants gave him an African funeral of sorts, placing his heart, intestines and other internal organs into an iron tin and burying them under a mpundu tree. They engraved the names of the people who were present on the trunk of the tree.

The King of Ilala summoned all the chiefs, men and women of his country to come out with their drums to mourn their Doctor in accordance with their customs; it was said that the drumming and dancing went on for two days.

Finally, a party of determined and brave loyal African porters, headed by Susi and Chuma, who were Livingstone's most loyal servants, set off with the carefully wrapped embalmed body securely tied to a pole and carried between two men at a time. They recruited other porters on the way. Among those newly recruited porters was my Grandad Mulutula. African porters trudged through deep forests, swamps and crocodile-infested rivers until, after six months, and having covered over 1,500 miles, they were able to pass the body into the safekeeping of the British authorities.

Jacob Wainwright, a Yao boy and a freed slave had been baptised and given a Christian name after being sold into slavery as a child. He had been sent to India after being freed from slavery. He became a pupil at the Church Missionary Society School where his subjects included English and Christianity. He joined Dr Livingstone's final expedition in 1872, and, as he was the only servant who spoke English, he was chosen to accompany Livingstone's coffin to England. Jacob was able to tell of many of the unknown details of Livingstone's travels and the circumstances of his death.

Anyone would think that such loyalty and persever-
ance, on a journey of hundreds of miles and many months,
would have been handsomely rewarded by the British government. Unfortunately, it appears that the opposite came
into play. Once they arrived in England, the African porters
were treated shabbily and received no compensation from
the British government.

Their status became unclear. People did not know whether
they should be treated as heroes or savages, whether they
were honoured guests or servants. Were they entitled to be
called explorers and discoverers of foreign lands, or was that
only for white men?

Much has been written about Livingstone's adventures
and is there to be read in the history books, but what you
are about to read is the story of how, if not for the Doctor,
my grandfather would never have become the respected
village headman, judge, healer, the champion of inheriting
deceased relatives' wives, a proud husband, father, brother,
uncle and a very special grandfather; the teller of many wise
and hilarious stories.

CHAPTER TWO

THE ORIGINS OF GRANDAD NGOSA KABASO SHOMPOLO MULUTULA

My grandad's oldest surviving blood relative is still strong and well at the wonderful age of 93. Mr. Peter Mulutula, living in Kitwe on the Copperbelt of Zambia, was able to tell me a lot of things about my grandad, who is now long gone.

Grandad Mulutula was born in the late 1850s at Shimumbi village, Chief Matanda, North East Zambia, which was then a British colony. He lived a long life, although it has to be acknowledged that during the Victorian era there were no official records for births and deaths for native Africans in British colonies, and as administrative duties were carried out by colonial masters, it is most unlikely that any true records about my grandad were kept. It's thought that he passed away in the late 1960s at Katobole village, Luwingu District, North East Zambia.

Grandad lived to a very old age which was no obstacle to his indulging in youthful feistiness and lust for life. Even at that ripe old age, he continued to be very strong, alert, and fully aware of place and time. He died a much respected elder who carried on being a comforter to many, as well as being a pillar of his community. Above all, he was able to move about unaided and could perform most of his daily activities quite independently. Grandad outlived his wife Lucia Mulala by a couple of years during which time the Mulutula adult children, their wives and his grandchildren kept an eye on him while he continued to live independently in his round, red-brick house.

Mulutula the Family Man

Following Mulutula's return from Impiwe in East Africa where he had assisted as a porter on Dr David Livingstone's Great Epic Journey, he married Chief Mulala's granddaughter, Lucia Mulala. His royal in-laws gave him wedding gifts of large portions of land. On one of the plots on the Itandashi River estuary, he established Katobole village. Mulutula and Lucia had three sons: my uncles Sakeni, Katinta and Samuel, and two daughters: Auntie Margarita (Margaret) and my mother Besa Milika Mulutula. After their deaths in the late 1960s, Grandad and Grandma were survived by at least four generations: their own children and grandchildren, and many great-grandchildren who in turn had produced children of their own.

Mulutula the Muscled Teenager

Grandad narrated to us grandchildren that, as a child, he was told that he had inherited immense fighting powers from his ancestors, and that these powers had emerged very early in his life. By the time he reached his early teens, he was more than six feet tall and had developed massive amounts of body muscle. In the area where he lived, he quickly became known and greatly respected for his skill in cutting down opponents with his massive, fiery blows. It is said that Mulutula used to frighten his opponents by calling out "*Ndekulutula!*" meaning "I will hit you hard!" For sure he meant what he said, and could beat the hell out of whoever tried to square up to him. This was how he got his nickname 'Mulutula', which means 'big hitter.' The name grew on him and later became his surname and family name.

Naturally, when Livingstone's entourage, which was ferrying the missionary-explorer's embalmed body to East Africa, passed through his father's village, he was an obvious recruit. This was how Grandad Mulutula's relentless entanglement in Dr David Livingstone's saga began.

The Great Epic Journey

Grandad explained to us as children that Shimumbi village, as his home village was known at that time, was situated along big plains near Lake Bangweulu. It happened to be located along the route Livingstone's entourage decided to use as a shortcut to avoid Lake Bangweulu in the west, and the Muchinga Escarpment Mountain in the east.

The distance between Chitambo in Zambia, where Livingstone had died, and Bagamoyo on the east coast of Africa was about 1,500 miles. It took African porters, including my grandad, six months to walk the journey, carrying Livingstone's body on their shoulders.

Grandad Mulutula's Bedtime Stories

As a little girl growing up at Katobole village, I remember hearing Grandad tell us children how he was recruited as a young man to join David Livingstone's entourage ferrying the Doctor's embalmed body to the east coast of Africa. From there it was to be shipped across the Indian Ocean via the Suez Canal and the Mediterranean Sea to his final resting place in the United Kingdom.

By the time the entourage reached Shimumbi village in 1873, my grandad was the most feared young boxer in the area. Presenting his bulging muscles, his charming good looks and standing at six feet tall or more, he became the colonial master's first choice for a porter's position, as he was perceived as a powerful young man who would withstand the punishing journey on foot from Zambia to East Africa.

Grandad told us how he and the other porters walked night and day carrying the remains of Bwana Munali. In October 1873, they encountered Lieutenant Verney Lovett Cameron, who had been sent by the Royal Geographical Society to look for Livingstone, who was presumed lost in Central Africa. Lt. Cameron insisted that Livingstone should be buried at Unyanyembe where he had met the African porters.

Constrained by their African humility and still in mourning for their beloved master, the Africans stood their ground and insisted on returning Livingstone's remains to his people in the United Kingdom and were determined to push on towards Bagamoyo.

Lt. Cameron became angry and left his friend Dr W.E. Dillion in charge. Cameron took Livingston's medicine and equipment and left alone. After an argument with other explorers over the source of River Nile, Dillion shot himself through the head. With the help of a small dog, the African porters gathered the scattered bone fragments and blown-up brain pieces before continuing their trek towards the Indian Ocean.

African Porters' Summary Dismissal

Despite their loyal and respectful intentions, the African porters were ill-treated and bullied by Lt. Cameron who wanted Livingstone's body to be buried at Unyanyembe, Tanganyika. As if being bullied by Lt. Cameron was not enough, when the African porters arrived at Bagamoyo with Livingstone's corpse, they were paid meagre wages and summarily dismissed by the Acting British Consul Prideaux. Female porters were discriminated against and were not paid any wages at all; among the women porters was Susi's wife.

The Wild Trek Back Home

Grandad Mulutula was one of the 79 dismissed porters who made the difficult trek back home. In the absence of travelling equipment such as compasses and maps, some of the returning porters wandered off into unknown territories.

The Rejected Royal Marriage Proposal

My grandad was one of those who wandered off and accidentally passed through Chief Mulala's kingdom. This was where he saw and fell in love with Chief Mulala's granddaughter Lucia. Mulutula made a marriage proposal to the young girl's royal family but it was rejected as it was assumed that Mulutula was from a low-bred family, and that he was a mere traveller (referred to as *bena fyalo*), with no money and no fixed abode.

Mulutula's Tenacity and Determination

Fortunately, Mulutula's tenacity and his determination to prosper helped him accept the rejection for the moment. He made his way back to his own village where he obtained proof to show to Chief Mulala that he was in fact a descendant from chiefs and that his father was a respectable village headman of Shimumbi village. Mulutula was then dispatched with the necessary dowry and marriage gifts, along with elders to escort him back to Chief Mulala to ask for Lucia's hand in marriage. Chief Mulala was impressed and allowed Mulutula to marry his granddaughter.

Chief Mulala welcomed his new son-in-law into his family and bestowed on him large portions of land where Mulutula established Katobole village which still bears the same name today.

Memorabilia

Grandad had one positive memory of the Great Epic Journey, having kept two colonial Scottish hats which were given to him as mementos. He treasured and cherished his Scottish hats and wore them at big events and ceremonies such as weddings and funerals, or when he was presiding over cases brought to him as village headman when he sat in court with his advisors at Katobole village.

CHAPTER THREE

KATOBOLE VILLAGE

As a royal son-in-law, Mulutula's status automatically changed and he quickly became a village headman, a traditional healer and a respected man of great wealth in his community. In the late fifties, right through into the early sixties, foreign investors flooded the area prospecting for manganese. The government showed interest and started mining manganese on a commercial basis. They built a battery factory at the nearby provincial town of Mansa. However, at that time the Zambian economy depended on copper production and they were ranked the third copper producer in the world. So manganese mining was not given any international recognition and when foreign investors packed up their equipment and left, manganese production was neglected and finally was forgotten. Surprisingly, sixty years later, the area around Katobole village is once again being flooded by foreign investors mining manganese ores. In short my grandad's village has once again gained its past glory. There is a lot of manganese mining activity which is a blessing to the people who live in the area, as this has brought them job opportunities.

My grandfather was a tall, authoritative person who was at the same time liked, feared and respected by his subordinates. To his family and wife, Grandma Lucia, he was a gentle giant who unconditionally accommodated and cared for his five adult children and the grandchildren they gave him. His favourite hobby or pastime was to tell stories to his grandchildren. Some were true stories based on his personal experiences and others were riddles based on fiction, yet full of wisdom and meaning, and they served as lessons against any wrongdoing in real life. As such, the grandchildren became accustomed to gathering together after the evening meal, and listening intently to his stories, which sometimes ran into the late hours of the night. Afterwards, the children retired to their allocated sleeping quarters in Grandad's round house.

Unstoppable Clatter

The name of Grandad's village 'Katobole' means 'unstoppable clattering or talking'. I am not sure of the origins of the name, but at the same time, this strange name does not surprise me. It was no secret that women from Katobole village talked or quarrelled nonstop. One of my aunties, Ba Mayo Bana Chibwe (the mother of Chibwe), or Auntie Margarita, was unstoppable. Nobody could put in a word once she started talking. Jokingly and affectionately, people referred to her as 'Umulabasa wa chalo chonse' which meant 'local radio'.

While writing the chapter on Katobole village, I rang my first cousin Mr Bonwell Katinta, son of my late Uncle Katinta Mulutula, to pass on my condolences on the death of his sister's son (whom I have referred to as one of Katobole's Fallen Stars later in this chapter).

Then I started asking my cousin about the origins of the name 'Katobole'. He informed me that his father, Uncle Katinta Mulutula was a merchandise trader who used to buy goods from Zaire (Democratic Republic of Congo), and that on his trips he used to stop over and rest at Katobole village in Zaire. Being an influential and much-travelled son, he managed to persuade his father, Grandad Mulutula, to rename his village 'Katobole'. Whatever it was that had been embedded into my late uncle's brains about the name I don't know, and my cousin said he did not know either why the name 'Katobole' was so important to his father, hence I assume only God knows. After all, Uncle Katinta's trade was similar to that of a sailor, so perhaps he left his anchor at Katobole village in Zaire and instead of going back to pick it up, he decided to sink one at his father's village where his actual family lived? This might have kept him connected to the memorable Zairean village and what he had left there. I was elated to get this piece of history from my cousin about Katobole village – a piece I had not known before.

Coming back to Katobole village itself, it grew very big, but in those days I perceived it as a small town. Our village had many houses, most of them built from burnt bricks. At that time, sons and nephews went out and married women from other villages and brought them back to Katobole village. Likewise, daughters and nieces found husbands who would come and settle at Katobole village. There were also other settlers from extended families who came to set up home at Katobole village. And of course there were Grandad's patients and their families who decided to move permanently to our village. Eventually, the village grew and grew until it became the hub of all the villages in the surrounding area.

Katobole village became famous for its joyful and spectacular street parties and organised dances that would be thrown with any flimsy excuse such as a wedding, Christmas or New Year celebrations. There were also weekly parties and monthly beer parties as well as lucrative money-spinning events such as Sandauni (a fee-for-entry party which started at sunrise and finished at dusk). Most of these activities were organised by men while the women would cook delicious dishes for participants and visitors to eat. There were also informal get-togethers. In some cases, parties were thrown to welcome relatives who had not been seen in a long time, or to welcome wealthy visitors from the Copperbelt, the mineral-rich region of Zambia hundreds of miles away. I remember it was always party time. On those special occasions, I would dash around tasting different dishes and occasionally join in the dancing. These were activities I would not dream of doing at my parents' home, as they were strict Jehovah's Witnesses who shunned any activity involving dancing and partaking in the consumption of alcohol, which to them was perceived as evil and un-Christian.

The Katobole Village Villain

Isake Chamutobo was Mulutula's nephew, only son of Chilekwa. He will appear in later chapters of this book as the family's black sheep; he was Katobole's jailbird, a devious and villainous character.

According to Uncle Peter, Chamutobo was the son of Chilekwa's second husband, Mr Stephen Kasosa, who was given to her through the local tradition of inheritance following the death of her first husband, Mr Ngelesani, Peter's father. However, Uncle Peter stated that his newly installed stepfather, Mr Kasosa was a habitual thief who he thinks passed on his criminal genes to his son Chamutobo. Uncle Peter confirmed that, as a result of Mr Kasosa's criminal activities, Chilekwa divorced him and later married Mr Maliwawa, and that the couple were blessed with three daughters, Keana, Mumba and Belita.

Meanwhile, Chamutobo had a colourful criminal career and was constantly being arrested and sent to various prisons in the country. When arrested, Chamutobo gave false names to the police – usually the names of other Katobole male residents. This meant that when the police came in their trucks to Katobole village in search of Chamutobo, innocent men would be harassed, arrested and brutally bundled into police trucks which attracted scenes of hysterical wailing and weeping wives and children of arrested innocent men. Grandad had to beg and explain to the policemen that the offender must have been his deceitful nephew Isake Chamutobo and not the innocent male villagers who had been apprehended and detained.

Chamutobo continued his criminal activities all over the district and surrounding provinces and it took a long time for the police to get to know and disregard his devious tricks. Finally, they came to know that Chamutobo was the hardcore criminal in the area who kept changing his name by impersonating men from Katobole village.

As mentioned at the beginning of this chapter, much of the valuable information about my grandfather and Katobole village came from Uncle Peter, Mulutula's only surviving blood relative. I have enjoyed many long and humorous telephone conversations with Uncle Peter, who, despite his advanced age, is as bright as a button. I am humbled by his personal genuine contributions which are pivotal to all reminiscences of Katobole village.

Katobole Village's Fallen Heroes

As explained earlier, when my grandparents passed away, they left at least four generations of Mulutula offspring. My mother Besa Milika outlived all her siblings and eventually passed away in March 2013, aged 88 years.

Meanwhile, whilst researching for this book I received news from Zambia that late Uncle Katina's grandson, Moses Katuta, had passed away aged 48. He was one of Katobole's shining stars. After holding senior jobs in various insurance companies, Moses became an affluent entrepreneur in Zambia. It was Uncle Katinta who gave the name of 'Katobole' to Grandad's village, therefore Moses was in direct lineage to Katobole village's heirs. At a tender age, Moses was one of the very few young Zambians who embraced the new exuberant entrepreneurship in Zambia and refused to migrate to other countries in search of jobs and wealth. Despite having a brother and sister permanently stationed in South Africa pursuing lucrative jobs there, Moses always said to me things like, "Auntie, you can continue living in England and let my brother and sister continue to live in South Africa, but for me I find living, working and running businesses in Zambia more attractive and worth pursuing."

I will always miss his enthusiasm, charm, his softly spoken manner, his faith in me – always praising the little things I do! He used to say to "Auntie Grace, you have done a lot of things for our family," and I would strongly protest to his nice sentiments. Hence I feel empty and I am in tears each time I think of Moses. I know he would have been so proud of me writing this book based on Mulutula and Katobole village. I know he would have said, "Auntie, this is very good work! You have put our Katobole village on the Zambian map," and then the two of us would have just collapsed laughing. Moses was my only nephew who looked after me when I was at home most evenings. After he had finished work, he made sure he passed through my Makeni home to check on me and my ailing mother before he continued to his farmhouse at Chilanga. I am singing praises to a fallen hero, a shining Katobole star whose life has been drastically cut short! We Katobole offspring will always look up in the sky to spot your shining star Moses; you will always be missed by all of us Katobole Village Successes.

To give credit to Grandad, many sons and daughters from Katobole village have produced very successful children. Some are engaged in middle- and high-ranking government positions in Zambia. Others have established themselves as academics or professional entrepreneurs. The writer of the book, for example, is a daughter of Mulutula's second daughter Milika Besa Mulutula, who herself was a Katobole product.

School Planting

When white missionaries arrived in the area and set up schools, my grandfather told me that they chose Katobole village as a place to start a school because of its strategic position on the estuary of the Itandashi River. The river officially marks the boundary on the map of Zambia between Luapula and the Northern Provinces in North East Zambia.

In those days, the late fifties and early sixties, many children, including myself, found ourselves at Katobole village because our parents had sent us to live with relatives in order to attend the Katobole village school. This was easier than staying at our parents' villages as it saved young children from the ten-mile commute to school each day.

On reflection, it worked to both children's and parents' emotional, developmental and social advantage. A large number of children at Katobole village grew up together as brothers, sisters, and cousins. In those days, we were so carefree and happy, and I remember being surrounded by many cousins; boys and girls. We used to eat together, go out to play together and sleep in my grandparents' house together. We never fought but we jealously protected each other from outsiders. The bigger ones fought any intruders who tried to disturb our peaceful pact and besides, we were the 'untouchable' grandchildren. We were even respected and feared by primary school teachers who failed to mete out any corporal punishment to us, as if they did, Grandad would march to the school and have a harsh word with headmaster, Uncle Mukundubili, who in turn would punish the junior teacher who had imposed punishment on any of the Mulutula grandchildren.

Innocent Indulgence

I truly enjoyed my stay at my grandparents' village and cried my eyes out each time my parents sent for me. I used to refuse and dream up an excuse why I should not go. My favourite one was faking an illness and I remember staying awake one whole night coughing and sniffing, deliberately letting my grandmother hear me. As a child, I would sometimes fall asleep but would jump up in my sleep and start coughing and sniffing loudly until Grandma woke up and came to check on me in the middle of the night. Afterwards I would allow myself to sleep soundly because I would have the assurance that my grandma knew something about my night illness.

I used to love it the following morning when my grandparents would say to whom ever had been sent to fetch me, "No, no, Bupe" (they called me by my middle name which is a direct translation of Grace) "...cannot go to her parents' today because she is not well." And my grandmother would say something like, "Ooooh, poor thing, she never slept the whole night, she coughed and sniffed all night long!" Then she would say, "I will boil some leaves so she can breathe in the hot vapour to get rid of that cold she has." Each time one of us caught a cold, my grandmother used to fetch fresh leaves from the nearest bush and boil them in a pot. Then she would take a blanket and throw it over the child with the hot pot full of leaves in front of them. Usually she sat under the blanket with the child and removed the lid from the pot. The child would inhale the hot, fragrant vapour, and after some time, would emerge from the blanket dripping sweat. I used to be so scared of being covered in the blanket with Grandmother and her hot pot, so I always tried to get better before she boiled her leaves. Later, when I was living alone with my family in England, far away from my relatives and their traditional remedies, I improvised the same treatment for my own children, except that I put Vicks Vapour Rub in hot water and then threw a cover over myself and my child and let the child inhale the hot vapour for a while. I tell you, it worked – especially during winter months; I definitely resorted to my grandmother's traditional remedy!

My second escape route was to hide my clothes away a day before I was due to go home to my parents for school holidays. My grandmother, when trying to pack my small case, would come out of the house in shock and say, "Oh my God! Somebody has taken all of Bupe's clothes; she cannot go back home dressed like that…" (pointing at me in my unflattering play clothes) "…her mother will be angry with me!" And she would interrogate everybody in the house as to where my clothes had gone. What she didn't know was that I had purposely hidden my clothes under her bed, knowing very well that she would not check there as she would not suspect that innocent six-year-old Bupe could think of such a mischievous plan.

It all ended with Grandma apologising to whoever had been sent to collect me. Grandma would say, "I am sorry I cannot let Bupe come with you, but tell my daughter Milika, I will bring Bupe myself when she gets better." Even before the messenger's shadow had disappeared from my grandparents' gate, I would burst out of the house like a bullet to go and join in whatever games the others were playing outside. My grandparents would sit there laughing their heads off. They could not believe that Bupe, who had lain limply on her sleeping mat the whole morning, had been cured to run so fast from the house after the departure of the messenger. Eventually, Grandma would run after me, begging me to eat something before I continued playing with the others.

I preferred being at Grandma's to being at home with my parents because there were so many rules, like having to bathe before going to sleep, combing my hair which was kinky and painful to run a steel or metal comb through, and cleaning my teeth using a small root or plant which tasted bitter in my mouth afterwards. Worst of all, my father being an elder in the Jehovah's Witness church, going to church was the pivotal point of any family activity – I found no joy in being sat or clamped next to another sibling on the bicycle's carrier with Mum cycling at high speed towards another village where church services were held. As if being bundled to church was not enough, we were banned from having fun with other children or joining in dancing sessions. Our dad wanted us to stay quietly at home and read, or help Mum with her errands. As a child, I thought it wasn't much fun; besides everybody was scared of Dad, and none of us would dare object or break his rules. Meanwhile, at my grandparents' house, there were no such rules and besides, I was treated like a princess. Grandma preserved the best food for me. For example, during the rainy season, she would show me where she had hidden special fruits like ripe mangoes, bananas and oranges. She would not allow other children to eat them, and I was the only one allowed to go and fetch one whenever I felt hungry. Accidents did occur sometimes though, when a naughty cousin would follow me and find out where I was getting all those fruits from. And then word would go round, and before my grandmother knew it, all the fruit had been eaten without a trace.

Grandma would only warn me and tell me to be careful, otherwise I would go without any fruit myself. She would continue in her soft voice and refer to my other cousins by saying, "They have their own parents here and they can eat from their parents' houses. You have no mother or father around, that is why I care for you most."

In those days, such beautiful, caring and loving sentiments from Grandma meant nothing to me. She used to speak to me with those gentle words while holding me on her lap, stroking my hair or creaming my hands and legs after a bath. However, I would just keep quiet without responding to her, and after she had finished straightening my dress or skirt, I would slip away from her gentle grip and run out to play with the others.

Now, as an adult and grandmother myself, I think about Grandma a lot, and sometimes I miss her and quietly cry for her. She loved me so much and yet she died without me reciprocating my love for her. All I can say is: may her soul rest in peace. I know she still watches over me and probably she is proud of her little Bupe who has turned out to sing her praises.

In my grandparents' village, I was free to do anything, such as playing outside until my feet were sore. Having said that, and as a grown-up adult, I must thank my late father for being such a disciplinarian. His positive attitude towards academic achievement has borne fruit to all his offspring. Even when he didn't have money in abundance, he sacrificed many things to ensure his children received a gainful education. Unfortunately, he did not live long enough to reap and enjoy the fruits of his investment in his children's education. It is not surprising that I am now writing about him with the utmost honesty and fondness, which gives me great pleasure and pride. I have such beautiful and priceless memories of him, all because he was such a generous and selfless man who was a self-taught colonial mine policeman-cum-semi-village entrepreneur who wanted his children educated.

Geographical Boundaries

Katobole village still bears the same name and is situated on the estuary of the Itandashi River which flows into Lake Mwamfuli which further joins the great lakes, known as Lake Bangweulu. On the map you can see that the Itandashi River forms a boundary between the Luapula and Northern Provinces. Although Katobole village is officially in the Northern Province, medical and educational facilities are fifty miles away in Mansa in Luapula Province. Mansa was, and still is, regarded as the nearest provincial town in the area.

The town's name comes from the mysterious Mansa River, which, unlike other rivers in the area, has no plain, but vast and deep flowing water runs on what looks like dry land.

Fort Roseberry, which was renamed Mansa after Zambia's independence in 1964, still bears some colonial symbols, such as a fort built for watching out for warriors advancing from Abercon, now called Mbala, a small border town built on Lake Mpulungu in Northern Province. Today, Mbala serves as a gateway port to neighbouring countries in East Africa such as Burundi, Uganda and Tanzania. Lake Mpulungu is a natural boundary between Zambia and East Africa, so the warriors that invaded Zambia came by ship via Fort Jameson.

Legend has it that Sir Roseberry and Sir Jameson met at Mansa and signed a declaration there to bring an end to the wars in the area, and the ruins of the fort where the two white men met are still there. Today, visitors pour in to see the ruins lying on the slopes just a few yards away from the glorious Mansa Hotel, a wonderful location for tourists and local visitors alike.

The Village Scandal

One year, there was a village scandal concerning an imbecile impersonator which sent shock waves through the entire village and set tongues wagging in all directions. This man, who was treated and perceived as a village imbecile, embarked upon a hot and sizzling affair with a prominent wealthy man's wife, whom he later married.

The story was that the unsuspecting village shop owner, thinking only of his wife's security when she travelled to faraway fields, asked Chekapu to escort his wife and provide company to the honourable lady. But the rich man's wife and Chekapu started an affair and the humiliated, cheated husband only came to know about it after Chekapu started to boast in the village of impregnating a shop owner's wife. Chekapu had become so confident and excited that he made such announcements each time he got drunk, which was on a daily basis. He would stand up and tell whoever wanted to listen that, although he could not afford to pay the Hut Tax, his status in the village should now change, as he had just proved that he was a man by impregnating so-and-so. At first, the other villagers would just listen and laugh as they took it all as a joke, but Chekapu's boasting became more and more regular until he became so confident and elated at his prowess that he began to mention the real name of the pregnant lady.

An Impromptu Hush-Hush Court Hearing

Katobole village went into a period of secrecy as the scandal involved one of Grandad's favourite sons, my Uncle Samuel. Grandad instructed that a court hearing be set up as soon as possible. Chekapu was brought to the village tribunal, headed by my grandad, to answer a charge of adultery with a married woman of higher status in the village. All Chekapu's bravado evaporated and he was so frightened and mortified that he shook like a leaf.

He appeared unable to stand unaided, and two men had to hold him up as he wept and begged for forgiveness. He thought that Grandad would send him to the white man's prison or ask him to swim across a crocodile-infested stream, as those were some of the judgements often imposed on village lawbreakers. The poor souls would languish in hostile prisons or perish in a crocodile's stomach without a trace.

Grandad, being the great statesman he was, summoned the woman's family to attend the court hearing as well. He wanted to hear the case from both sides. Before passing judgement, Grandad conceded that his son was partly to blame for entrusting his wife to the care of a man of low status who naturally had low morals and would do anything, oblivious to the possible outcome or repercussions such as the disgrace he had brought upon a respectable family.

Addressing his daughter-in-law, Grandad called her a woman of low morals who originated from an impoverished and cursed family lacking any cultural dignity. Their daughter was born and raised in dire poverty, but she had had the good fortune to be heralded into noble high status by marrying into the Mulutula family. Grandad should have known the saying which states that "you can take a person out of the ghetto, but you can't take the ghetto out of the person".

The disapproving and enraged Mulutula recommended that the offending pregnant daughter-in-law should go back to her family who should, in turn, hire Bana Chimbusa's wise marriage counsellors to impart some wisdom and teach her about the kind of behaviour expected from a married woman – especially one who was married into a respectable and ruling family.

The poor woman had no defence. In those days, things were dealt with differently. Today, she could have asked for a DNA test to be carried out; after all she was still living with her husband at the time of her pregnancy. Who knows, there is a possibility that, despite her adulterous affair with Chekapu, the unborn child might still have been her husband's. In spite of all Grandad's wisdom, it appears the entire judgement was based on nothing more than allegations of Uncle Samuel's wife having had an affair with another man. In the absence of any proper legal representation, the judgement was based on probability and not factual evidence.

Grandad instructed his son to divorce his disgraceful wife; he also instructed, by way of damage limitation, that Chekapu was to marry the pregnant lady on the condition that both of them leave Katobole village immediately and settle somewhere very far from the respectable Mulutula family. Grandad gave custody of the woman's two children to Uncle Samuel, hence my mother's younger brother was left with the burden and embarrassment of bringing up his own two boys. Nobody ever talked about nor knew what happened to his first wife and the imbecile's child.

The Beautiful Bride

Uncle Samuel remarried a few years later, this time to the most beautiful woman I had ever set my eyes on. Rumour had it that she had come from the Copperbelt. My new Auntie Veronica dressed so graciously, like a princess, that each time she walked along the village streets it seemed like she was dancing on air, her feet not touching the ground. Her elegance gave Katobole village reason to be so proud.

Unlike my previous auntie, she never went into the fields but served in Uncle Sam's village store where she proudly sold commodities to excited customers. I am sure some men and women came into the store just to steal a glance at Katobole's new beautiful bride.

The Will

Many years later, and long after I had emigrated to the United Kingdom, my now-late brother wrote to me advising that the youngest of Uncle Samuel's two boys, who had grown up to become a senior police officer, had passed away. My brother also informed me that my cousin had left a will in which he had left some money for his wife and children, as well as to my mother, his auntie, as by then both his mother and Uncle Samuel had already passed away. I was really surprised as I had never even thought about those boys until my cousin's kind bequest of naming my mother in his will. May his soul rest in peace.

K-A-N-D-O

A good friend of mine, a daughter of a village school head teacher in Luapula Valley, now living in the UK, makes me laugh when she tells me her childhood stories. She has a story about one of the village imbeciles in Kashiba village, nicknamed K-a-n-d-o by the local children. He was a short man who wore tattered khaki shorts and torn T-shirts. As a self-appointed Catholic, he wore an improvised big wooden crucifix around his neck. According to my friend, Kando was a very naughty boy with a foul mouth who yelled insults at people who tried to engage with him – especially children and teenagers who teased him and purred his name as K-a-n-d-o each time he passed by.

His antics would always reach a climax on Sunday mornings when the whole village attended mass. Kando would cause mayhem by walking into church late. He would then purposely make a scene at the entrance of the church by kneeling down in an exaggerated manner, making a spectacle of himself by hissing out prayers whilst grasping his large wooden cross in both hands. Then he would slowly stand up and begin a long slow walk up the aisle, while the whole congregation sat and watched.

Kando would be dressed in his purposely shortened shorts, with the zip at the front deliberately broken. His wooden cross swung around his neck. He would glide slowly up the aisle, stopping every now and again, cocking an ear for the children's whispers of "K-a-n-d-o! K-a-n-d-o!" then he would stop abruptly, look around until he spotted where the whisper had come from, then he would unleash his big bomb of an insult aimed in the direction from where the whisper had come! The congregation, especially the children, would then burst into uncontrollable laughter.

Toronto

Most villages and towns have their own imbeciles or village idiots, but I clearly remember one such man I met at Mansa in Luapula Province, north-east Zambia where I went to attend my younger brother's funeral in 2008. This young man had renamed himself Toronto. The story goes that he was born with learning difficulties in Lusaka, to a Lozi mother who abandoned him. Catholic missionaries took care of him, bringing him up in various orphanages. In his teenage years, he was taken to live with Catholic priests at Mansa, but apparently Toronto later rejected the Catholic way and started to wander and sleep rough. Cleverly, Toronto took to entertaining gatherings at funerals where he could eat and drink for free!

It was therefore not surprising that Toronto turned up at the Chama family funeral house and he was not disappointed, as somebody had whispered to him that one of the mourners had come from England. Toronto introduced himself to this fellow foreigner. He explained that he was from Canada, hence his name Toronto, which, he said, was evidence that he was not a local boy, but somebody from abroad.

The same day, Toronto started making comical advances and marriage proposals to my younger married sister. This was a most inappropriate marriage proposal which, in spite of the solemn occasion, had everyone, including the close family in mourning, laughing their heads off.

Although Toronto was a simple-minded individual, he possessed hidden talents which were not even known to him. It was widely rumoured that he possessed strange diagnostic powers and could predict an individual's medical prognosis, which proved correct in most cases. For example, it was reported that whenever he visited Mansa General Hospital, he did his rounds, selecting certain patients and telling them how long they had to live before they died. In most cases, what Toronto predicted happened; patients would die on the exact date he had predicted. His visits therefore frightened and petrified patients who would try frantically to run from their hospital beds, despite their critical health conditions, because Toronto's predictions seemed to be their death sentence.

As might be expected, the authorities took steps to permanently ban Toronto from visiting Mansa General Hospital. Toronto was devastated but that's how it goes when it comes to the harsh law of the jungle. I have often wondered why some kind of professional investigation wasn't carried out to verify Toronto's ability. His diagnostic talents could probably have been tested and put to good use under proper medical supervision.

A story which really caught my interest was the one where Toronto stood up in a church service one Sunday morning and shouted at the priest. The sermon was about morals, and the priest had said that the worst sinners were adulterous individuals. It was then that the infuriated Toronto stood up and called the priest a cheat and a traitor. He proceeded to loudly inform the congregation that he had seen and witnessed that very priest having a tryst with one of the nurses! Of course, Toronto was very quickly and roughly thrown out of church for raising such a rumpus.

Fuming, embarrassed and feeling dejected, Toronto vowed to prove to the congregation that he was not creating stories but telling the truth. He therefore set out a calculated plan in which he waited until nighttime when the accused priest drove to the nurses' hostel and parked his car in the hostel's car park. Toronto vandalised the valves of the car tyres, letting the air out of all four tyres. Then Toronto went and knocked on the door of the visiting bishop, telling him of an incident concerning one of his priests. Toronto then led the bishop to the priest's car.

Toronto, satisfied that his plan was working, went upstairs into the nurses' hostel, and knocked on the door where he knew the priest was with the nurse! He called the priest's name, telling him that something had happened to his car. Upon that, the story goes; the pyjama-clad priest came charging out at Toronto who fled swiftly down the stairs. The priest pursued him out into the car park, only to see the bishop standing by the side of his car with its flattened tyres. The cheating priest was suspended and finally expelled, to the satisfaction of Toronto who became an overnight hero, and from that day on would receive free food and drink from excited housewives and men of good morals.

Heirs to Katobole Village

Uncle Peter later confirmed that the offspring of Mumba Tebulo are the current inhabitants of Katobole village, where they continue to live, although both parents are long gone. The Tebulo children and grandchildren have maintained all the traditional features of Katobole village, including its name.

Uncle Peter told me that his deviant half-brother Chamutobo died of old age a few years ago. Uncle Peter, who has five adult children of his own, also confirmed that Chamutobo had no children known to members of his family, so it is believed that Chamutobo left no heirs to Katobole village.

CHAPTER FOUR

THE HIDDEN HEALING CLAY POT

My grandfather Mr Ngosa Shompolo Mulutula was a village headman and a traditional healer. Grandad specialised in healing people with mental health problems. He had a big clay healing pot which was hidden in the bushes on the outskirts of the village. As children we sometimes used to sneak out and go into the bushes looking for the big clay healing pot.

Legend has it that Grandad took his patients and their grown-up relatives to this sacred place where he would boil leaves and roots in the clay pot and later administer medication to his patients. To this day, I do not know whether Mulutula's patients drank or bathed in the boiled solution of medicine.

Having said that, most of Grandad's patients were mid or late teenagers or young adults in their twenties who had succumbed to mental illnesses, hence they were strong, agile individuals who sometimes presented themselves as challenging, agitated, virile and aggressive towards children. As a result, children were not allowed to witness any of the healing sessions.

However, one morning, the elder boys conspired amongst themselves and recruited the younger children to go out to the thicket and look for Grandad's healing pot. We started off and walked for hours in tall grass, not even thinking of snakes, or the cuts to our unprotected legs we were getting from the razor-sharp grass. Suddenly, one of the bigger boys who had ventured deep into the thicket came out panting and shouting that he had seen the black healing pot. He was shaking and trembling and not lucid at all. We all ran towards him, some falling over the overgrown potholes on the ground. One of my cousins ran fast and grabbed the back of my neck, shouting at me not to go near the medicine pot nor touch it. He said if I did, I would go blind, and then I would go mad. Ugh, I jumped back onto the foot-beaten path and waited for further instructions. By then, my heart was doing somersaults in my mouth, throbbing wildly in my chest. My throat was getting dry, I could feel heartbeats in my ears and I was slowly feeling giddy, as I though I had already touched the black clay pot.

I must have lost my balance and passed out, because the next time I opened my eyes I was in Grandma's house and I saw Grandma in a kneeling position touching my forehead. I momentarily thought, *what have my cousins told Grandma? Should I tell her the truth?* Where could I start because I was already afraid of the telling off I would get. So I kept quiet and let Grandma use her usual traditional medication for high temperature which consisted of sitting under a blanket with the pot of boiled leaves.

After making what seemed to be full recovery, I did not like to hear anything regarding Grandad's black healing pot and I never ventured in the direction of the thicket where my other cousin said he saw the healing pot.

Grandad's Grateful Patient

Grandad once told us a story of how he came face to face with one of the young men he had helped to recover from a mental illness. He said that after many years he had forgotten he had been hired to treat a young man who had succumbed to a mental illness. He said when he reached the young man's village, he felt touched and mortified to find this young man had been locked up in a hut and chained down in a wooden canoe-shaped box. Grandad spoke of how he got angry with the young man's parents for treating their own child like an animal. He ordered the parents to release the young person and started administering medication to him. Unknown to Grandad, the young man had recovered so well, he got married and migrated to work in the copper mines. Grandad continued to tell the story of how, on one of his visits to the Copperbelt, he went to a town where his relatives worked, and where his young ex-patient also worked and lived. Grandad said his male relative knew the young man as they belonged the same tribe and came from the same area. Hence Grandad's relative had unknowingly invited the young man to come and meet the visiting uncle from the village.

Grandad said the young man could not believe his eyes – that he was meeting the very man who had rescued him from the hut where he had been imprisoned and had helped him recover from a mental illness. Grandad said the young man bought him clothes and gave him a new blanket and some money. On top of that, the young man told Grandad that his wife was expecting their second child and that he was going to name the unborn baby after his famous traditional healer. This young man's gesture of honour both surprised and humbled him. Grandad gave his blessings there and then but also requested that the young man bring the baby named after him to the village so he could give his personal blessings to his namesake. We teased Grandad and asked how a girl could be given the name of Mulutula? Cunning Grandad assured us he had given the young man and his wife permission to choose from his names of Ngosa, Kabaso, Shompolo and Mulutula. We agreed with him and said yes, probably a baby girl could be named Ngosa or Kabaso and a baby boy could either be called Shompolo or Mulutula. This goes to show that Grandad had his moments to show his sense of humour to his inquisitive and ever-challenging grandchildren.

The Unscrupulous Traditional Healer

During my book research, I was told of an unconfirmed story that took place in rural Zambia. It was reported that a young woman was once taken for treatment for mental illness by her parent to a traditional healer. However, the traditional healer's treatment method consisted of placing a red-hot clay pot on the patient's head to drive away evil spirits. Legend had it that the young woman was left with first-degree burns – gaping head wounds inflicted by the red-hot clay pot on her scalp. Eventually, she had to be rushed to hospital for treatment. Nobody could confirm to me whether the young woman survived or died from her burns.

Unfortunately, when I asked the whereabouts of the traditional healer, or whether he was reported to authorities for inflicting first-degree burns to the woman's head, nobody was willing to give such information as they were probably fearful of repercussions from the traditional healer and his family in the event that he got caught, prosecuted and sent to prison.

Dr David Livingstone on African Traditional Healing

Writing on Dr David Livingstone and his legacy, Dr Marion A Currie states that Livingstone was deeply interested in the culture and practices of the people among whom he lived. She further states that "Dr David Livingstone was tolerant and observant of the practices of the traditional healers and he regularly agreed to try their remedies on himself." *(Livingstone's Hospital* p.252)

Dr Currie further states that "Dr David Livingstone thinks that, although the native prescriptions are often sufficiently absurd, there is reason to believe in the efficacy of some from their being widely known among various tribes and over vast territories."

The Livingstone Pill

Compared with other explorers in Africa, there is evidence that Livingstone lost comparatively fewer men on his expeditions. His remedy for fever was as follows: "Resin of jalap and calomel, of each eight grains; quinine and rhubarb, of each four grains. Mix together well and when required make into pills with spirit of cardamoms. Dose – from ten to twenty grains. The violent headache, pains in the back etc. are all relieved from within four to six hours; and with the operation of the medicine there is an enormous discharge of black bile – the patients frequently call it blood. If the operation is delayed a spoonful of salts promotes the action. Quinine is then given till the ears ring, etc. We have tried to substitute other purgatives instead of the resin, jalap and calomel but our experiments have only produced the conviction that aught else is mere trifling." The remedy became known as 'The Livingstone Pill'. *(Livingstone's Hospital* p.252)

CHAPTER FIVE

AFRICAN VILLAGERS' HUT TAX

Katobole village did not escape the suffering and fear inflicted on African villagers as white colonial masters toured collecting the African Village Hut Tax.

All African men over the age of puberty were expected to pay a quarterly levy to the white colonial administration which was operated from the District Commissioner's offices in various sub-BOMAs in each province. This word became the common way of speaking of the British Overseas Management Administration, and government in general.

In Grandad's village, the days before the arrival of the white tax collectors were marked by various energetic cleaning rituals. Men repaired and made new roads through the village. They also created lawns and flower beds around their houses. New roofs were put up or old roofs were mended with fresh neat thatch. Overgrown fences or shrubs were nicely trimmed, usually demarcated with planted sisal, or ulunsonga. They also built and dug latrines for each household. Women smeared the floors and walls of their houses in various shades of clay: white, yellow and red for the outer house walls and black for the floors. Most interior walls were washed and painted in white lime, or *inswakala*, which was probably made from local powdered white marble. There was also another type of white clay powder called *impemba* which was dug out of deep river banks; the red powder, *nkula,* was made from the bark of a specific tree which the villagers planted for this purpose. As most houses were made from burnt bricks, the painting was restricted to the lower walls of the structure, whereas those houses built of mud walls were fully painted using the coloured clay.

During those times, Katobole village could easily be mistaken for an urban compound such as those seen in today's big towns. The village inhabitants were expected to wash and dress themselves smartly and ensure that their children were also dressed in clean clothes. The entire village took on a carnival-like atmosphere, resembling Christmastime. The women were ordered to cook their meals in improvised kitchenettes, just for that day's exercise. These enclosures had to be hastily built as nobody was allowed to cook on open fires, as was the normal village practice.

Insaka, the Communal Male Shelter

When they were not working, the men and teenage boys would gather in a communal shelter, called *insaka*, where they would eat their meals and also play games like isolo, which today we would know as draughts, and something similar to snakes and ladders. This shelter too was renovated and re-thatched.

Insaka was also used to tell stories about manhood and the elders used this time to impart their wisdom and knowledge to the upcoming young men of the village. There was a 'Bemba' proverb: '*Imiti ikula, empanga*' which translates as 'Growing children are the future of any society'.

I always wanted to sit with Grandad at insaka and listen to those wise, funny stories which made everybody laugh so much. Unfortunately, as a girl, I was not allowed to sit there, but I always volunteered to take Grandad's meals to him and then I would purposely drag my feet on leaving so I could eavesdrop on any stories being told. Usually, my male cousins knew my tricks and would shout out for me to leave at once, which I did, sometimes in floods of tears. I seriously wanted to hear those stories as my male cousins refused to disclose the subjects they discussed with the elders. One of them told me that doing so would cause him to be perceived as a coward, or a man influenced by women and under a 'petticoat government' which is not allowed in African culture.

Another reason I used to envy my male cousins who were allowed to eat with adult men at insaka was that I thought they had access to a lot of food. The wives would cook or prepare meals for their spouses and bring it to insaka where the teenage boys were seated, chatting or playing games with the older men.

However, one disgruntled male cousin told me that young boys were not treated well at all when it came to sharing meals with the adults. He said the youngsters were refused food by the elders who used very flimsy excuses to exclude them from sharing meals with them, especially if the meal consisted of meat, chicken or fish. When it was a poorly prepared meal or it was 'nshima', which is like a thick porridge made from cornmeal, with beans or vegetables, then all the boys would be invited to eat with the adults.

Some boys complained to their mothers about the treatment they suffered at mealtimes in the insaka, so their mothers would leave portions of food for them to eat in the evenings after retiring from the insaka. Some wives realised that their husbands too were just not quick enough to compete with so many hungry men and boys who fiercely attacked any meal. So the clever ones would leave favourite delicacies for their husbands to eat in the night. Who can blame such clever women! They kept in mind another traditional proverb: 'You can only keep a dog under your roof if you give it enough food'. The women would remember their *bana chimbusa's* wise counsel to newlyweds of ensuring that the husband's stomach never goes empty – whether that is for food only, or any of the husband's other daily or weekly bodily needs.

The Village Idiots

There was another feature which surfaced at the time the colonial tax collector was expected at Katobole village. Unknown to the white administrators, Grandad Mulutula used to discreetly instruct poor men who could not afford the Hut Tax to turn themselves into village imbeciles, or completely disappear from the village until the colonial entourage passed.

The trick worked as follows: a day before the advance party arrived, the poor men who thought they could not afford the levy took off their everyday clean clothes and clothed themselves with rags made from old sisal fibre. They smeared their bodies in red, black or grey dirt from the ground, and sometimes improvised their disguise by using ashes collected from the women's fireplaces. The results were very convincing – I remember one man in particular, Mr Chekapu Chiboboka, who I really believed was mad. I never went near him because of his regular disguises which, to my child's eyes, assured me that he really was an imbecile.

The Advance Party

Ahead of the white tax collector's visit, the menacing 'kapaso' or messengers would descend on the village like vultures, full of showiness and brandishing their guns. An air of fear and expectation would sweep the entire village as the kapaso, usually dressed in khaki shorts and short-sleeved khaki shirts, made their way through the village. They wore big off-white khaki hats with strings tied below the chin. The kapaso's uniform included thick black socks, or 'imp atishi', a big buckled belt and mountaineers' boots.

The kapaso would stare at the disguised imbeciles who by now would have positioned themselves strategically along the roadside, looking slyly at the kapaso, bemused by the pomp and excitement. In the meantime, the gun-toting kapaso would start to shout insults at the imbeciles, pointing their guns and rudely telling them to move away from the roadside or else they would have their stupid brains blown from their foolish skulls.

Those messengers looked mean, deadly, intimidating and ready for action. They waved their guns about like children playing war games in the fields. There was good reason why the kapaso were feared, as they were known to sometimes overreact and abuse their powers by burning down houses or kicking anything which seemed unacceptable in their eyes. It could be an old man coiled in fear between two huts or a sick dog slumped on a door step. When in full action, the kapaso continually shouted insults in the Afrikaans Cikabanga language. Sometimes I could understand or guess a few words as my father had been a colonial policeman and sometimes used the language at home when reprimanding us children. When my father spoke this foreign language, we thought he sounded very educated and sophisticated! So we understood why the kapaso used such a highly respected language only spoken by their white masters.

From my childish viewpoint, I thought I saw the kapaso pause or stop every now and again, threatening to kick or beat up the imbecile who took too long to make a move before the white man's arrival. With a show of exaggerated anger, the kapaso would instruct Grandad to do something about his mad men or else the kapaso would burn down his entire village. In response, in an exaggerated but very solemn voice, Grandad would ask his poor mad fellows to move away and leave the roadside for the white tax collector's entourage. And obediently the disguised men would disappear until it was safe to return.

Party Time

With the District Commissioner's departure, the whole village could breathe a sigh of relief. The men who had become imbeciles while the tax was being collected would have gone to the river to wash the dirt and paint from their disguised bodies and then reappear well shaven and in clean clothes to join the party which, by then, would be in full swing. Women would bring brewed beer and cooked dishes, mostly leftovers from food served to the District Commissioner and his entourage.

What I didn't know then was that my grandfather himself had come up with this plan to protect and save his poorer people from paying such heavy duties to the colonialists. By choosing a few men to disappear and a few others to turn into imbeciles for a couple of days until the District Commissioner completed his tour of the surrounding villages, he saved the people from hardship. However, who could blame my grandfather for doing so? To me, Grandad Mulutula was an intelligent, genius, village headman.

The Generation Aftermath Effects

There was one not so pleasant outcome from the plan which still persists today. It is that some of my generation still tease those whose parents pretended to be imbeciles in order to avoid paying their tax.

For example, on one of my frequent visits back home to Zambia, I met a man who had prospered and done very well for himself, in spite of his family background. As a gesture of goodwill and to celebrate our childhood days, the businessman invited me and a couple of other individuals from our village to an evening out. The evening went very smoothly, however, when everybody was relaxed and a little bit tipsy, the conversation turned to childhood stories, and one of them was about the mystery of the village imbeciles during the District Commissioner's visits to Katobole village.

Our host, the big businessman, became a little nervous and became very defensive of his father. However, one of my outspoken friends insulted him by reminding him of his roots, and even telling him that he was not fit to possess the kind of wealth he had, and that it should have been given to her, because she came from a family who had paid the required taxes.

Surprisingly, our host took such criticism very calmly and reminded my big-mouthed friend that although she came from a family of higher status than his, she had spoilt her chances of reaching a position of power by neglecting to develop herself academically, and that she had rushed into a poor marriage. He also reminded her that she did not have the intelligence for any higher achievements, but instead had been gifted with a big nasty mouth to insult anybody in a position of power. He told her, "The only cure for your curse is to find very strong chemicals to purify yourself to become decent enough to be welcomed into the homes of the higher flyers – which is the only way you will ever be able to walk in the corridors of power!"

Sensing danger and further embarrassment from the edgy discussions, I hastily joined in. I reprimanded my big-mouthed friend for humiliating the children of men who were unfairly dehumanised by the practices of the notorious, racially-motivated colonial regime.

I reminded her that our host was a living example that one can come from the most modest family backgrounds and yet make something out of his or her life. There is no limit to what one can achieve in life, given the opportunities.

I sincerely apologised to our host and congratulated him on his business knowledge that had led to his accumulation of vast wealth. I earnestly encouraged him to join mainstream politics and make some valuable contributions to the improvement of our village, as well as to the entire country. My apology was accepted and the evening ended very amicably thereafter, thank God!

CHAPTER SIX

CHENGO THE BESTOWAL

Since my childhood, I have been intrigued by the story of one of my ancestors, Chengo. She had a 'rags to riches' story, and when I was older, I asked my mother if I could rename myself after this strong and brave girl. My mother agreed shortly before she passed away in 2013, and thereafter she always addressed me by the name of Chengo. I always cherished my mother's kindness in allowing me this honour, which had been my childhood wish. This is the story she told me about my ancestor who became a princess:

Many years ago, perhaps as long ago as the 1700s, Chengo ran away from her home in Cherubic Island and managed to cross the wide, crocodile-infested Bangweulu Lake on her own, eventually reaching the mainland on the other side. It is not clear exactly why she chose to run away from her immediate family, but Chengo had heard stories from her parents of another branch of the Bena Mbulo clan who had settled on the mainland, and her intention was to find them and go and live with them. These people lived in an area called Mulumbi village, which up to the present day still bears the same name. Chengo knew that the head or chief of this family was known as Mulumbi Chandashika.

However, things took a turn which prevented her from continuing on her journey to her clansmen, and which is the beginning of the story of her lineage.

When Chengo arrived on the mainland, she asked for directions to Mulumbi village where her clansmen lived. A young man advised her to go and see the paramount chief of the area before she continued to wherever she was going.

Tired, hungry and confused, Chengo was probably also feeling frightened and extremely vulnerable, but she took the advice of the young man. What he had not told her was that, when visiting a paramount chief, a visitor should bring gifts in the form of gold or other valuables such as new blankets, mirrors, alcohol, cattle or even human beings. These tokens were given to the chief as a sign of respect, and such gestures would raise the visitor's status in the eyes of the paramount chief. It was also expected that whoever presented the paramount chief with the greatest gift or bestowal was presented with a piece of land or could be allowed to marry one of the chief's own daughters or nieces.

Unaware of this, Chengo humbly followed her guide who led her to the palace of paramount chief Chungu. On arrival, the guide, who according to my mother's account was nothing more than a trickster, or *cimambala,* managed to talk his way through to the main building. In those days, a paramount chief lived in a fortified compound called an *icipango,* and access to the chief's compound was through one gate manned by the chief's *kapaso* or guards. Although he had no status, the guide must have been a crafty but intelligent person to persuade the guards to allow him an audience with the chief.

The guide and the frightened Chengo were eventually ushered into the chief's reception area where visitors of lesser status were received. When they reached the room where the paramount chief was waiting for them, the guide and Chengo knelt down and bowed. Whilst in their bowed position, the guide, who was as terrified as Chengo, started to greet the chief with a lot of exaggerated praises:

"Everlasting Chief, the greatest of all kings, I humble myself to you as your obedient servant, and greet your honour with utmost respect. I am ashamed for coming to see your honour without gold or cattle. However, I present to you, your Lordship, 'a lost soul' who I found on my travels. She is young, pretty and pure and will serve and attend to all your honour's natural wishes and needs and wants with the utmost respect and tranquillity."

Her head still in a bowed position and her eyes closed, Chengo could not believe that this man, whom she had trusted as her guide, had just given her to the paramount chief as a gift. She started sobbing uncontrollably.

Unknown to Chengo, the paramount chief had been looking at her intently from the time the two entered the room. The chief raised his hand and, addressing Chengo directly and in a most sympathetic voice said, "Have you got anything to tell us, little one?"

The chief's intervention was most unusual as, in those days, the chief did not speak directly to a subject, or find himself facing a lost frightened girl; the norm was for the chief to address the subject through his advisors. Chengo, finding an inner strength, grabbed the opportunity and spoke up. She opened her eyes and, through her tears, she protested at what the guide had said. She told the chief that she did not know the man who had brought her to the palace and besides, she was not lost at all. She had come from Lubumbu in Chilubi Island and she was on her way to go and visit her clansmen and women who lived at Mulumbi village in Chief Mulala's area.

In response, the paramount chief ordered the *ba mushika*, his advisors, to get the full story from the beautiful girl who seemed so pure and genuine. At the same time, the chief dismissed the guide's story and ordered him to be thrown out of the palace with immediate effect. The story goes that chief Chungu ordered his guards to punish the trickster in accordance with the rules of the land. Who knows what happened to him? My blood goes cold in my veins when I imagine what fate this man met, for in those days, rulers were harsh and there was no pardon even for the smallest offence. Whether his offence was termed as kidnap or the trickster had been labelled as a perpetual liar, both offences might have been punished with a life sentence or death by beheading or being thrown to hungry lions.

Chengo was later led to special rooms where other women cared for her. She was given food and clean clothes and was allowed to rest while the paramount chief gathered more information regarding the authenticity of his new visitor's story.

A few months went by before the paramount chief was satisfied that the young Chengo was indeed on a mission to visit her clansmen and women in senior chief Mulala's area. The head of that clan, Mulumbi Chandashika, was summoned to the chief's courts and questioned at length to confirm if he had any knowledge of other branches of the family. Chandashika testified that he knew of people living on islands scattered all over Lake Bangweulu.

According to my mother's account, after his interview with the paramount chief and learning of the plight of a virgin girl who had been presented to chief Chungu, Mulumbi Chandashika went back to his kingdom and met up with his elders. The clansmen and women donated gold and other treasures and sent wise men back to Chief Chungu's courts to request the release of their clan's virgin girl Chengo who had been detained there.

The paramount chief's response to Mulumbi Chandashika was sharp and direct. He told them that Chengo was not held in captivity at all, but that he, the paramount chief, had made up his mind that Chengo should be looked after and cared for by his people at his palace in harmony and tranquillity.

Within days, the paramount chief announced that he had decided to marry Chengo to senior chief Mulala of the Bena Mukulu people, who had no wife and was lacking heirs to the throne. This decision must have been the most exciting coincidence to Chengo, whose original intention was to seek out her clansmen and women who lived in Chief Mulala's kingdom. Was the paramount chief reuniting Chengo with her intended relatives or was it that he, the paramount chief, genuinely wanted to have this brave, beautiful little girl become a princess and give heirs to one of his senior chiefs? Somehow, this was the best thing that could have happened to a runaway islander on a mission to find the relatives she had never known.

A few days later, Chengo was dispatched to Chief Mulala's district where she became the young wife of senior chief Mulala. For the first few years, her new clansmen and women were happy to receive the young princess as she brought royal connections to her new adopted family, which naturally raised their status. They automatically became direct in-laws of a senior chief, so a dowry and other precious marriage gifts were presented to Mulumbi Chandashika and his family.

However, a few years later, an evil twist started to emerge for Chengo. The very clansmen and women she had adopted as her family became viciously jealous of her royal marriage which had given her fortune and high status. The clan's elders undermined her position by persuading senior chief Mulala to take on a second wife. According to my mother's account, Mulumbi Chandashika chose his niece to be married to chief Mulala.

Of course, the new development upset Chengo intensely. How betrayed she must have felt by the very people she had come to live with as her own family. By all accounts, Chengo's position was weak in that she had no blood family to support her. Also, it is likely that she was threatened by her adoptive family that if she put up any resistance to her husband taking on another wife, she would be divorced, or even killed.

Up to this present day, I can clearly imagine the vulnerability and deep emotional betrayal that Chengo suffered, and I try to fight for her through my own life. I speak to her and try to give her support and encouragement – I always whisper to her to be brave and strong. I tell her that even today the injustices she endured still exist – wealth and success inspire enmity and jealousy from one's own family! I think about what happened to Diana and other strong women of this century. Diana's family envied her so much that in later years they never spoke to her. As for the singer Madonna, her own brother published cruel stories about things he claimed she did during her childhood. What could a Victorian woman do in such circumstances, with no education, no religious faith nor parents to rely on? Her life at that time must have been intolerable. I sometimes weep silent tears for her in the night. Having no family of her own to rely on while her husband was being enticed by a younger woman and encouraged by the very people she trusted must have made her immensely depressed. For the sake of saving both her life and her marriage, she had no choice but to allow her husband to take on another woman against her will.

Chengo had given birth to three girls. Chungu Mulala was the eldest. The second, Chabala Mulala, was unfortunately deaf at birth. Katebe Mulala was the youngest. However, Chengo never gave birth to a boy who would have been heir to the throne. It wasn't until the next generation that an heir was born when her daughter Chungu gave birth to Mulala (my grandmother) and a boy Matiyabu, who by tradition would have become the direct successor to the throne.

But Matiyabu disappeared under mysterious circumstances. My mother told me that Matiyabu was a naughty boy and he was sold into slavery and was never heard of again. However, there are other even more unpleasant versions of what happened to him.

None of Chief Mulala's other wives gave birth to a male heir to the throne. The fact that Chengo had a grandson created an atmosphere of jealousy and resentment in the chief's house. Other women became envious and plotted to get rid of Chengo's grandson at any cost. The story goes that Chengo left to escort her husband on a royal tour of his district. Being the senior wife, it was quite normal for her to be able to leave her orphaned grandchildren in the custody of the other wives. Surprisingly, when Chengo returned from her royal tour, Matiyabu was nowhere to be found. The other wives would not tell her the truth, until finally one of the chief's advisors told her the whole truth about her grandson being sold into slavery whilst she had been away.

My mother told me that Chengo never recovered from this heartbreak, and became very withdrawn. She died fairly young. But the cause of her death is as mysterious as her arrival from the islands. One far-fetched story was that Chengo choked to death on her pipe. But did the other wives murder her and then come up with a story that she had choked on a pipe? Was Chengo a smoker? Was her husband Chief Mulala implicated in Chengo's death? Was she poisoned by her servants?

Nobody has given me any answers to these questions which keep bothering me. One day I will find out the truth and then I will put Chengo Mulala's spirit to rest.

Interview with Chief Mulala 7

Whilst in Zambia in April 2012, I was blessed to meet up with His Royal Highness Chief Mulala 7 who had arrived in the capital city, Lusaka, for consultations with the government.

Being a descendant of Princess Chengo, wife of Chief Mulala 1, I was granted my request for an audience with the current Chief Mulala 7 with no problem. The interview took place in a motel where the chief was staying.

I had no need to worry about what to wear nor how to greet the chief. I had known him from childhood as he had been my late brother John Chama's best friend when they grew up together as teenagers at Mulumbi, now renamed Museba Village, Luwingu District, Zambia.

What I saw when I reached the motel was this stunning, handsome, immaculately dressed man, who spoke with a crisp English accent. Before I even thought of my practised curtsy, this film star lookalike walked forward and hugged me! Oh God, I did not know chiefs gave hugs to their subjects. He commented on how grown up I was and how dignified I looked – so it worked both ways – there I was admiring his good looks and good spoken English while he was commenting on my sudden change into a dignified woman. We shyly looked at each other and laughed like awkward teenage lovers.

His Royal Highness informed me that he was born Ronald Chungu Chisumbu on 10th October 1943. He worked as a miner in Kitwe for many years. He was installed as Chief Mulala 7 by Senior Chief Chungu of the Bena Mukulu tribe on 11th August 1999, following the death of his first cousin Kapulo, Mulala 6. He also confirmed that since the reign of Mulala 1, who failed to produce a male heir to the throne, inheritance to the throne had switched to maternal heirs such as sons of sisters and nieces of the reigning chief. The chief further explained the origins of his title or ceremonial name of 'Kalume Kepi' ('short boisterous man'). He advised that as part of tradition, any installed chief had to choose a name or title he wanted to be addressed by his subjects. He said he chose Kalume kepi munshitina mabumba which means 'a short courageous man who is not intimidated by large crowds nor gatherings'.

His Royal Highness commented that his relations with the Zambian government had greatly improved. In regards to his people, they still remain loyal and respectful to him. While he spoke of hounding the government for more schools, health centres and a post office, his biggest wish at that time was to source funding for a ceremony to be held at the Senior Chungu official palace in September 2012.

In conclusion, his Royal Highness in his charming, engaging tone said, "I believe that the appointment to become a chief is a destiny given by God." We thanked each other and parted on friendly terms after exchanging cordial pleasantries, only this time I gave him a full curtsy farewell.

CHAPTER SEVEN

BESA THE RUNAWAY BRIDE

My great-great-grandmother Chengo left her home on Chilubi Island and crossed the great lakes on her own to the mainland where she knew nobody. She knew only of clansmen and women whom she had heard about in the folk tales told by her parents.

They say that history repeats itself. Three generations later, my own mother Milika Besa Mulutula also had to run away from home. In my mother's case, it was a forced marriage which triggered her rebellion.

Chengo became mother to three daughters, the daughters of Chief Mulala: Princesses Chungu, Chabala and Katebe. The eldest daughter Chungu married and she in turn had two children, Lucie and Matiyabu. Unfortunately, Princess Chungu died at a young age, leaving the two children as orphans. Their father had been chased away years before by Chief Mulala when it was discovered that he belonged to the Bena Mbulo Clan, which was in fact Chengo's clan, therefore he was related to his wife's mother and should not have married Princess Chungu. Even in those days, clanship was taken very seriously and marriage between people of the same clan was not allowed; as we know today interbreeding can cause problems with offspring.

So, my Grandma Lucie and her brother Matiyabo were brought up by their grandmother Chengo Mulala, with assistance from their auntie Katebe Mulala, the youngest of Chengo's three daughters. Many years later, after Lucie had married Ngosa Shompolo Mulutula, she wanted to thank her Auntie Katebe Mulala for bringing her up. So they offered their daughter Milika Besa, my mother, as a bestowal (impokeleshi) to Katebe's husband, Mr Kasonka.

Unfortunately, or fortunately, young Besa (my mother) ran away and was kept hidden by her deaf grandmother Princess Cabala until the wedding ceremonies to her grandfather were cancelled. After which Besa met this dashing six-foot handsome man (my father) whom she married. People can conclude that this act of defiance and liberalism from a teenage girl in the 1930s has been passed on through genes to her daughter who happens to be strong-willed and a woman of intellectual prowess.

Ironically, when Grandma's father was chased away, he married into another chief's family and produced children whose sons were in line to inherit the kingdom.

When my Grandma Lucie died in the early seventies, Chief Chisunka (to whom she was related through her father's second marriage) sent mourning gifts of blankets and money. As a little girl, Grandma used to tell me that she was related to Chief Chisunka but I took no notice. Probably I was too young to understand the whole issue of clanship then.

But the clan relationship is still recognised today, as was proven when my brother retired from his various government jobs, and decided to settle at Mansa Boma in Luapula Province. He approached Chief Chisunka for provision of a small area of farmland and was well received as the grandson of Lucie Mulala, who was the daughter of Chief Chisunka's ancestor. It's true; blood is thicker than water, especially in Zambian circles.

Coming back to the two orphaned children, Lucie and Matiyabu; Katebe Mulala had no daughters of her own but had two sons, Aaron Katuta and Sobingi.

The story goes that Chief Mulala had only daughters from all his wives. However, he had a grandson, Matiyabu. Traditionally, a male in the family would inherit the kingdom, hence Matiyabu became the rightful heir to the Mulala kingdom. But Chief Mulala had other wives who were infuriated by this and conspired to sell Matiyabu to Arab slave traders while his doting grandmother Princess Chengo was not around. So Matiyabu received his rightful heir-ship to the Mulala kingdom as he was taken away into slavery. As mentioned above, this episode led to Princess Chengo's premature and unexplained death.

During my grandmother's generation, any son-in-law who proved to be a good man would be rewarded with a virgin girl from the wife's family. This was regarded as a mark of respect. The first wife became the chief wife (Mukolo) while the youngest wife was regarded as the child bearer, and in most cases was answerable to the chief wife and was expected to carry out all the household duties until such time that the husband took on another wife. That might be at the time when the second wife was no longer able to produce children. This practice ensured that the chief's lineage would continue. As a result, one man might father thirty or forty children in his lifetime.

In Africa, the more children one has, the more land one cultivates. Having many children came to symbolise wealth and prosperity. Parents of many girls for example, may accumulate their wealth through dowry payments. On the other hand, parents who produced many well-educated boys were assured of a future of wealth and prosperity from their offspring. Hence having a good number of both girls and boys was and still is a bonus and a sensible 'investment' for any parent on the African continent.

According to my mother, it broke her heart that her parents, who had refused to send her to school because she was so beautiful, had decided to marry her off to an old man. She decided to rebel against their decision and ran away from home a few days before the marriage ceremony took place.

Besa sought refuge at her second grandmother's house – Chabala Mulala, who unfortunately was deaf. As a result of Chabala Mulala's hearing impairment, nobody in the family thought of questioning her, let alone suspected she would hide the rebellious runaway bride. As days and weeks passed by without anyone knowing where Besa had run to, the family gathered once more and resolved that Besa should not be made a bestowal to Mr Kansoka after all; instead, another virgin would have to be found immediately. When word went round and reached Besa where she was hiding, she decided to go back home and rejoin her angry and anxious parents, regardless of whatever punishment was in store for her.

However, a few years later, Besa fell deeply in love with the young, dashing, tall and handsome man whom she knew through her younger brother. My mother told me that this young man, called Jairous Chama Katebe, came to their village to meet her brother Samuel Mulutula so the two young men could travel together to the Copperbelt to look for paid jobs. In those days, the 500-mile journey from the Northern Province took more than two weeks on foot. These days, the same journey may take a few hours by air and at least six hours by car. A bus journey still takes a day or two, depending on the state of the vehicle.

The story goes that the two young men remained good friends, and after getting himself a job as a native mine policeman, Jairous, who had boasted and teased his friend Samuel on their trip that he would marry his sister, decided to honour his promise. He travelled back to the Northern Province to marry Besa Mulutula whom he later brought back with him to Mufulira Mine where he was working.

I am the sixth child of this loving couple's marriage. On reflection, I have always felt like congratulating my mother, who even in those days had such a strong liberal attitude towards choosing a partner. I always wonder what would have happened to me if my mother had agreed to marry her grandfather. Probably, I would never have been born or I would have been born as a different person altogether.

Mum, I still salute you. You are the greatest mum in the world. As I always say to you, thank you for your bravery and for having me, as well as for passing on to me some of your natural characteristics such as extraordinary bravery and tenacity, an easygoing personality, as well as the gifts of charm and the ability to inspire others.

CHAPTER EIGHT

MIXED BLESSINGS

There was an atmosphere of celebration; after all it was only three days after Christmas and most people were still nursing their hangovers or complaining about their persistent stomach aches.

It is not a secret to say that there are quite a number of traditions characterising the festive period in the Christian world; the period from mid-December to early January.

Many Christians celebrate the birth of Jesus Christ by carrying out prayer vigils in churches, however, children and adults alike anxiously await their Christmas presents, and some believers and even agnostics embrace Christmas by drinking alcoholic spirits or wines. However, the norm of the entire Christian period is to tuck in to delicious roast dinners for which some start making arrangements months in advance.

One wonders what the fuss over Christmas is all about. Is it not the birth of Jesus? Why don't people just pull out their Bibles and pray? Why should we be obliged to buy presents for each other when we only ought to be doing so for Jesus, the son of God and our saviour? I can imagine how it felt to be in mourning on 28th December when every single soul in the land was still celebrating Christmas. Who wants their Christmas dinner marred by tears or the sorrow experienced by a neighbour or family member? Christmas is a time of joy, marked with prayers and pleasant gestures of giving and receiving. Everybody wants to join in festivals and street parties, and most of all it is a time of family reunions.

Mother Nature adds her own beauty to Christmas time. For example in the Western world, most people look forward to a 'white Christmas' where the land is covered in snow and all the households glitter with Christmas decorations. In Zambia by contrast, Christmas time is best remembered for its persistent rains – it can rain nonstop for days. Whenever the sun shines, the streets are filled with excited street dancers pursued by children and adults who have come out to celebrate Christmas.

For a young couple, Besa and her husband Jairous Chama, this rainy December day was to bring both deep sorrow and extreme joy to their doorstep. And thereafter, 28th December was to be an important day for their sixth daughter who arrived in this world at the time when her parents were mourning the death of their fifth daughter Eva.

My parents Besa Milika Mulutula and Jairous Chama were blessed with nine children, three boys and six girls. Unfortunately, three of the girls died in their early infancy. However, the writer is one of the surviving three girls and the couple's sixth child.

Bupe Mambepa Grace Chama made a rather agonising entrance to a world in which Besa and Jairous were still mourning the passing away of their fifth daughter Eva. Any mother or father will struggle to welcome a newborn baby on the day they have lost a child.

Could Grace's birth be perceived as a mixed blessing? Not to my mother, who years later told me over and over that she was not in any mood to give birth on the day when her beloved Eva passed away. She told me that she had to be restrained from hitting her stomach, not wishing to have another child at all. My mother said she was surprised that she went into labour immediately after Eva's burial, and that she gave birth to a baby girl. When I was older and I quizzed my mother about how labour pains felt, she told me that she was so grieved that she was beyond feeling any physical pain. However, what my mother meant was that the emotional pain she felt at suddenly losing her three-year-old daughter suppressed any physical pain.

Obviously, the new baby came at the wrong time. I can imagine the bonding process could have been difficult. My mother said she was feeling guilty, that she did not want to replace Eva and forget all about her, while on the other hand she was happy that God had blessed her with another girl. I naturally summarised her feelings as 'mixed blessings'. On reflection, I did not take my mother's feelings as a rejection of me, especially after becoming a mother myself. I shudder at the thought of losing any of my own children. God forgive us, in my mother's era, child mortality in Zambia was very high. I feel blessed to have brought up my four children in England where there are excellent medical facilities and the chances of any child living into adult life are almost guaranteed.

My mother once told me that in a moment of madness she decided not to keep the baby. However, the elderly midwives who delivered me would not tolerate such nonsense; they persuaded her to have a second look at her lovely baby girl before she made such a drastic decision. In most African customs, sometimes subtle loving feelings are not openly expressed. For example, one might expect a midwife to be very sensitive and tender towards a mother's feelings towards her newborn baby. Oh no, African traditional midwives would come in very strongly and command the mother to feed the baby there and then, regardless of how she felt. Tenderness and loving gestures follow after saving both the baby and the mother.

In my childhood, both my mother and my grandmother taught me a saying by which I have always lived and applied to my own children: 'You have to hate to love'. In other words, you have to be strong and firm in order to achieve your goals. Sometimes a soft approach hinders progress and fragments the intended objective, especially when you are dealing with children's education. African culture dictates that a parent has to be firm and direct with his or her children in order for them to achieve their academic goals. Another African saying is that you do not have to wrap your child, husband or wife in cotton wool, meaning that you do yourself no favours by spoiling or covering up for the wrongdoings of somebody you love or care for.

However, on that sad day, my bereaved mother did as ordered by the midwives, and one glance at the newborn baby made her change her mind. She said she saw light around the baby. She said the little bundle was so calm and innocent.

She said that in her eyes, the baby looked so beautiful it was unreal, which is why she decided to name her baby Mambepa, meaning 'too precious to last', the middle name was Bupe, a gift from God, and Grace which meant spiritual beauty and graciousness. However, my mother should be kicking herself because this Mambepa has lasted long enough to tell this story! It goes to show that she was truly a gift from God as she was aptly named.

It was not just my unusual birth that was to impact both my childhood and adult life, but the way in which my mother praised her late, beautiful daughter Eva.

As a child, I felt ugly and second best. As an adult I felt guilt for taking my late sister's place. These feelings led me to feel I needed to over-compensate my mother who had lost her daughter because of me, even though in truth, my birth had not caused my sister's death. I began to take on two roles in caring for my mother. Sometimes I imagined what my sister would have done for my mother had she lived, then I started thinking about what contribution I should offer to my mother on my sister's behalf.

I remember during my childhood my mother showed me, or rather pointed to, an overgrown graveyard and said it was the resting place of her beloved Eva. In rural Zambia, cemeteries are not cared for and therefore become overgrown bush within a few months or years. However, people still view such areas as sacred and there are many myths and tales of ghosts, bushfires and voices emerging from old graveyards.

However, my lasting wish has always been to erect a tombstone on Eva's grave while my mother is still alive. I feel this gesture will please my mother who lost her beautiful daughter at such an early age. For my part, it will be a sign of respect for the older sister I never had a chance to know. Through this sad turn of fate, I feel Eva has inspired me to pursue my dreams to achieve my academic and economic goals.

I always wonder what Eva would have achieved had she lived. Would she have been an academic, or would she have been competitive like me? How would she have looked? Would she have been forced into an early marriage and never advanced in her education? I know I will never get any answers to these questions. All I have is this image in my mind of a beautiful three-year-old whose sudden death broke her mother's heart, and in a strange way paved a way to the circumstantial birth of her little sister!

CHAPTER NINE

THE BLIND BEGGAR
AND MY LITTLE FISH

I n Africa, children start to provide for their families from an early age. For example, in my grandfather's village, children as young as seven or eight went out fishing and came home with enough fish to provide their families for a couple of days. Older boys escorted hunters who went out hunting animals at night, using big torches. Girls as well as boys would accompany day hunters who used dogs to chase and kill smaller animals usually found in thickets near rivers. Older girls helped with meal preparation, childcare, and caring for the elderly members of the family. Older women went out into the fields, and were involved in other activities like pounding grain such as maize or cassava, millet or rice, to make the flour for *nshima,* which was a kind of thick porridge that we ate with our main meals; they also helped with drawing water. These days, most big villages have been provided with water standpipes.

One summer evening after eavesdropping on my cousins' conversations about their fishing trips, I conspired to join them on a trip to Itandashi River where the group intended to catch fish in the morning. However, my cousins insisted that I remain at home as fishing was perceived as dangerous. Apart from the risk of drowning, when heavy rains caused rivers to flood, there were other dangers such as snakes, crocodiles and leeches. Frogs and many other water inhabitants were disturbed and could be clearly seen floating, diving or swimming in a dangerous flooded river.

The leeches would attach themselves to open wounds. In those days, most of us children had bruises and scrapes all over our bodies which we sustained from climbing banana, mango, lemon or pawpaw trees. Hence getting into the river attracted the leeches that could smell blood from our open wounds.

There was also an old myth or superstition that if a leech were to find its way into a girl's private parts, she would never bear any children as the leech would suck all the blood from her womb. That myth frightened the hell out of me and I was the last person to be coaxed to step into the river, and that was only after I had satisfied myself that my underwear was as tight as possible, leaving no space for any slippery leech to penetrate where it shouldn't! Of course, I was scared of the pain that I may feel, but I also hated the slimy and slippery fluid around the leeches – uugh, that was repulsive!

However, after revealing my wish to go out fishing with the group, I knew I had another hurdle ahead of me; how to convince my grandma to let me join the trip. I knew she would not allow me to go with the group so I decided to keep it secret and pleaded with the others not to let Grandma know. After realising that they were still reluctant to accept me, I took things into my own hands and made a fuss out of the whole thing. I started crying and throwing tantrums until my cousins gave in – and that was after warning me sternly that Grandma should have no suspicion of my intentions until we returned home with fish to present to her.

The big plains of the Itandashi River turned into small lakes during the rainy season. Usually there were strong currents which came with the flooding and these were strong enough to sweep away wild animals as well as human beings. Fishing therefore was a hazardous adventure, especially for children. Watching from a distance that morning, I saw men catching fish using nets and paddling away in dugout canoes. I also saw women, some with babies on their backs, catching fish using special baskets called *uluanga* in deep waters which came to their hips. I felt stunned as I watched this colourful scene unrolling before my eyes. It was like something out of the movies and I congratulated myself for having come out fishing with my cousins.

We saw children sitting fishing on raised river banks. The process involved using a steel hook, or *insande* (hook), which was tied to a long rope, which in turn was attached to a dried bamboo stick. A piece of fresh worm was attached to the hook, which was then cast into deeper waters below the bank. Within seconds, swarms of fish would rush to eat the worm, and in the process a fish would find itself hooked. The struggling fish would pull violently on the string attached to the pole, and the person holding the stick would automatically pull both the string and the hooked fish out of the water.

Anyway, we set off on our fishing trip after escaping the watchful eye of my grandmother who was busy sweeping inside the house. We carried enough food to keep us going for the whole day. Being the first time I had gone fishing, it was confusing for me as everyone wanted to give me instructions on what to do and what not to do. Sometimes my cousins would disagree on a point and this would leave me not knowing what the correct procedure was and I felt worried that I would make a million mistakes through being ill-advised.

The Itandashi River formed a boundary between two provinces and was therefore used as a highway to access villages in either the Luapula or the Northern Provinces. The plain itself was almost two miles long and small lakes would form on both sides of the purposely raised banks. A long, high bridge had been constructed where the river was deepest, but at its narrowest point.

It was exciting and interesting to see people, some walking, some riding bicycles, and even motor vehicles using the same highway across the river. To the present day, this route across the bridge remains popular and is still used the way as it was during my younger days, although modern improvements have probably been made in order to access schools, health centres and villages on either side of the river.

On this particular day, children and a few adults lined the banks fishing, using rods and hooks, while others waded into deeper waters, scattering nets. It seemed to me like a playing field full of people involved in various activities. My cousins joined them and had some good luck, catching a lot of fish. As time went by, I started thinking that I knew what to do and pleaded to have a go at it. After a couple of protests, one cousin agreed to prepare a rod for me. I was scared of worms and could not bring myself to cut it into pieces, let alone thread it onto the hook.

However, I followed instructions, and holding tight to the bamboo pole, I cast out the hook. I was just about to stand up on my feet when I experienced a big pull towards the water below. I cried out, and my cousin grabbed the bamboo stick from my hands and pulled at it with all his strength. And there was a fish dangling in the air in front of my eyes. I could not believe it had happened so quickly and that I had just caught a fish for myself! I ran towards the fish that had landed a few feet from where we were standing, but stopped almost immediately as I saw it lying there opening and closing its mouth, gasping for air with the hook still implanted in its mouth. My cousin ran after me with the instruction not to touch it as I may get hurt. I stood there in a trance waiting to see what the next step would be. My cousin slowly unhooked the fish, killed it quickly and handed it over to me. I took it and placed it on my small plate which had been empty until that point. I felt so proud of myself and wanted to run home to show Grandma, but then I realised that I had to catch some more fish before I could go back home.

However, celebrations were soon cut short by a commotion at the far end of the river bank. It so happened that a blind man, accompanied by his little son, was travelling in the opposite direction and was about to pass on the side of the bank where my cousins and I were fishing. Unlike the practice in developed countries where visually impaired people use a white cane or a guide dog to lead their way, in Zambia it is normal for a little boy or girl to act as a guide to their blind parents and lead them wherever they need to go. (In Zambia and maybe even in other African countries, young girls and boys act as guide dogs to their visually impaired parents.) I didn't know then that many of my childhood experiences would embed themselves deep inside me and I would write about them many years later.

As the blind man and his son walked along the river bank, he jokingly teased the children, asking them to give him their fish. These provoked different reactions from the fishing children who thought he meant what he said. Some ran away, others tried to hide by sliding down the banks. Of course, they knew that he could not see them. All I knew, when I looked up from admiring my little fish on the plate, was that there was a sudden commotion of children shouting to each other to run away or hide, while older ones shouted abuse at the blind man. I was confused and stood fixed to the spot. I remember wondering why an old man was holding on to a small boy. I also could not understand why everyone was running and shouting. I felt one of my cousins pushing me forward to get out of the blind man's way but I could not move and my legs felt like jelly. I could not slide down the river bank either as I was scared of the water. I looked down and saw my only fish on my plate and I thought to myself, *No, no, I won't run away and leave my only fish unattended.* So I stood there not knowing what to do, with the blind man hovering over me. The noise got louder and louder as my cousins shouted at the top of their voices to the blind man to leave me alone.

As though I was dreaming, I heard this boisterous voice saying to me, "Little one, give me your fish!" Amid cheers and boos, I thought to myself, "What next? Is he going to hit me or grab my fish?" And then I thought, *Before he does anything, let me give him the fish.* I bent down and picked up the fish from my plate and stretched out my hands to give it to him. I heard the little boy say to him, "Dad, she is giving you the fish." The blind man smiled widely and said to his son, "What? Where is she?" He lifted his hand as though to touch me. I thought quickly of stepping backwards but I knew that with one step I would fall head first into the river, so I stood still with my little fish in my hand. I must have gone into a trance as all I could feel was his hand touching my head as he said:

"This girl will always be blessed; she will have plenty in life and will never be short of anything. God will guide her life as she has a good heart." And then he said, "Your parents must be proud of you." Stretching out his hand, he said, "Here, please keep your fish."

By then all the children had gathered around and were both cheering and booing. In confusion, I dropped the fish back on the plate and started crying. Then there was dead silence and all I could hear were my own sobs. Then suddenly there was chaos as all the children rushed to give their fish to the blind man. The children kept shouting at him, "Here, here uncle, take my fish and bless me!" But the blind man only smiled and said, "Keep your fish, I was just joking, I do not need your fish."

He started to walk away but then he turned around and said, "Look, you have scared the little girl and now she is crying. Would you look after her for me?" And finally he waved goodbye and he and the little boy disappeared along the riverbank.

This is just one of the small incidents which happened such a long time ago, but remains stuck in my mind and has been a positive influence on my life. I remember telling the same story to my own children; some of them dismissed it, thinking I was being superstitious. But to me, it fulfils the saying that: 'One has to empty his/her basket before it gets filled again', or that: 'A person who gives away his precious ornament will receive tenfold'.

I can't help asking myself whether the blessings I received in childhood from the blind beggar on that river bank so many years ago have influenced my adult life. If not, why of all careers which were open to me did I choose to pursue a social work pathway? Was this my chosen destiny or total coincidence?

CHAPTER TEN

THE MYSTERY SCHOOL DAYDREAM

It all started with Grandma reminding us grandchildren to behave properly if we wanted to start school that year. Anything we did might affect whether or not we would be enrolled, so everybody would be on their best behaviour at the beginning of the new school year. In my case though, I knew I was too young to be enrolled and I had to wait a few more years. This really frustrated me! I used to sit there eavesdropping on the other children's school stories: about whom they had met at school, how they had learnt how to write their names and their parents' names. I grew desperate to go to school and could not wait for my turn.

Entry assessment for enrolment was conducted by the head teacher, who happened to be my uncle, Mr Philip Mukundubili. And because most children, and probably even their parents, did not know the exact ages of the children, my uncle had to ask each child to raise his or her right hand above their head, and if the child managed to touch the ear on the other side of their head, then they qualified for first year enrolment at school.

These entry assessments were taken so seriously that a few days before the new term started, children and their parents would camp in the school yard from dawn. They would form queues around the main school building waiting for the head teacher to come and make his assessment.

School enrolment day had its own special festival atmosphere. Parents ensured that their children were properly dressed and well-groomed, while teachers in their best suits would pose in front of parents and their children, sometimes chatting up young mothers on any lame excuse. Reflecting back on those days, I am sure the parents were more terrified of the teachers than their children were. They wanted their child to be enrolled at school at any cost, which was why they made such a great effort to be at the school from the crack of dawn to be first in the queue.

I realise now that Africans value their education more than anything else. Fathers engage in menial jobs in order to pay school fees for their children. Parents even sell possessions and land in order to supplement the fees. It's no secret that even today, most people of African origin working and living abroad still send funds back home to support the education of their extended families, my generation included. It's not that these people earn more abroad, or that they have less to pay for; it's just the African culture to assist and give support where it is needed. We are taught to share things from an early age, and if one gets a good job, such an individual is bound to help the entire family, often by assisting with the payment of children's school fees.

My family was lucky because the school was in our village and the head teacher was my uncle, so he automatically knew who was enrolling for each new school year. However, there was also competition between the parents who were anxious to have their children enrolled. Katobole village was big and everyone was related to the headmaster so he had to deal with the problem of satisfying family members before considering outsiders for available school places. Parents were so desperate to ensure a place for their children that I am sure there was also a lot of banter and bribery going on.

I overheard a conversation about my sister enrolling at the school and I saw an opportunity I couldn't let pass me by. Hence, I made up my mind that I would follow Josephine (my elder sister), who was more or less five years older than me, on her first day at school. Grandma had taken my sister for her school enrolment two days before the actual classes began, and for the next two days I cried in my sleep, wishing I could be enrolled as well. I started practising waking up early so I would not be late for school. I also started going to sleep early in the evening, even missing out on Grandad's story telling. At that particular time, I just wanted to prepare myself for school, even though I knew that I was not enrolled and no uniforms had been bought for me.

Finally, the day before the start of the new school term came and I went to bed early, or what I had thought was early evening and yet it was still afternoon. A few hours later, I woke up, and could not see my elder sister. I started panicking and crying hysterically – I thought that Josephine had left me and gone to school with Grandma. I ran outside the house still bawling, calling her name and asking through my tears why she had left me. I did not realise that it was actually late afternoon and that I must have gone to sleep immediately after the midday meal! Everybody came running towards me as I cried and threw myself on the bare ground not knowing what to do next. I thought my sister and my grandmother had betrayed me in such a bad way. My male cousin Bonwell was the first one to reach me. He pulled me up from the ground where I was still thrashing about and kicking my feet uncontrollably. He pulled at me, shook me hard and placed me in a standing position. Looking at me intently he kept asking, "What is the matter? What is the matter with you? Did you have a bad dream?" It was only when Grandma appeared and held me in her arms and started wiping off dust from my dress that I realised where I was. It was embarrassing to look at all those faces staring at me in amazement, with no idea what was happening to me. Maybe they suspected that I had been bewitched in my sleep. Out of the blue, everybody started laughing. However, it was not that funny to me because I had seriously thought that my sister and Grandma had gone to school, leaving me behind.

After that episode, I went back to my normal routine of going to bed after Grandad's story telling sessions. At least I was assured that it was the right time to go to bed, and so I did not experience any daydreaming again. On reflection, my first school daydream was due to my anxieties about going to school, when I knew very well that it was not my turn to start school yet. But as usual, I was a spoilt child who got what she wanted and not what she needed.

Mind you, that kind of behaviour was only expressed at my grandparents' home. I was definitely a different child at my parents' house. Both my father and my mother refused to tolerate any nonsense from anybody. Loving parents they were, but it was not a secret that no child was allowed to throw a tantrum at their house. And whoever dared got maximum punishment which deterred others from indulging in silly behaviour at any cost.

Katobole Primary School was situated on higher land on the other side of the village and Grandma's house was on the slopes leading to the Itandashi River; most of the village was built in the valley. The school had its own compound consisting of an impressive L-shaped building which was divided into different classrooms. There were also three or four teachers' houses. Unmarried teachers shared rooms in one house so there were fewer houses for a bigger number of teachers. The head teacher, Mr Mukundubili, was a fierce disciplinarian. He did not tolerate nonsense from any child. In those days, teachers were treated like small gods and were feared. So if a child misbehaved at home, all the parents had to say to their naughty child was that they would report his bad behaviour to Mr Mukundubili. Overnight, the child would change his behaviour to save his skin from the punishment he might endure at the hands of the teachers.

Because the head teacher was my uncle, I took liberties. Although my sister Jo was almost five years older than me, I decided to accompany her to school early each morning. Once in class, I would refuse to go back home and insisted on sitting next to my sister and would listen intently to the teacher. The class teacher would report this to the head teacher, but my uncle would just laugh over it and ask the junior teacher to continue teaching. Perhaps both my uncle and the teacher thought I would get tired and leave the class at some point and go back home. Yet I would sit there for hours, to the annoyance of my elder sister Josephine, who knew that if she dared to chase me out, I would throw a nasty tantrum and disrupt the entire class. She was not at all happy with me clinging onto her in class as the other children started laughing at her, and some called her names such as *kaboyi,* mother-child or nanny.

Those remarks, especially from the boys, used to embarrass her, and on reflection I regret putting my sister in such a dilemma at such an early age, as my actions affected her school performance. She felt challenged by her younger sister and failed to show her full potential in her schoolwork. She became an introverted, shy and insecure child. She was an average pupil in class and was not as outstanding as I was at that age. Everybody, including the teachers, noticed how bright and intelligent I was. Apart from schoolwork, I loved sports as well, which was rather a fun mixture; I played netball, I ran races, I competed in long and high jump. In fact I seemed to enjoy and indulge in absolutely anything which was thrown at me.

As if my sister Josephine hadn't endured enough, her troubles were not over. When we reached Standard Three (our fifth year), our father decided to send us to a boarding school run by the Anglican Church. As a result of our father's sudden illness, for which he needed treatment outside the country, it became difficult to raise the required school fees of £9.00 per child for both of us. Hence my sister Josephine remained at home and was married off while I was sent away at the age of eleven to Chipili Girls' Boarding School to pursue my education.

CHAPTER ELEVEN

GRANDAD'S DELICACIES

The Delicious Dish of Kalulu, the Hare Retrieved from a Dead Python

My baby sister, who was still little and stayed with my mother while all of us older siblings fled the nest, has vivid memories of things that took place at Grandad's village that she has shared with me whilst researching for material for this book.

Between the two of us, myself in England and my baby sister in Kalulushi, Zambia, we have managed to recall some lovely memories of our grandad whom we both remember with love, pride and joy.

My favourite story is the one she told me about Grandad having a feast of a dead hare, or *kalulu,* in our local language, retrieved from the stomach of a dead snake.

My sister related that one morning the teenage boys from Katobole village, who had gone to check on their rabbit traps, found a large python, or *ulusato,* which had swallowed something and now seemed unable to move and was stuck in the same position. The boys took big sticks and stones and started attacking the snake to kill. When they looked more closely, the boys became alarmed and suspicious about the contents of the snake's tummy as it was extremely large and swollen. They started shouting and calling for help as they thought the python might have swallowed a small child from the village.

Grandad, in a nearby cornfield, heard their shouts and the commotion, and from a distance watched the boys to see if they knew what to do next. The boys who had found the snake did not want to witness the snake's tummy contents on their own, but after a lot of encouragement from bigger boys who had come to see what all the noise was about, the snake's stomach was gingerly cut open and inside was found the carcass of a whole hare which had been the python's lunch. Amidst shouts of jubilation, they decided to remove the hare and either bury it or give it to the village hunting dogs to eat.

In the meantime, with his hands held behind his back, (which was his spying posture), Grandad hurried to the field where the boys were still debating the eventual disposal of the dead hare. He stopped the boys in their tracks and commanded them not to throw away the dead hare or give it to the hungry hunting dogs. He reprimanded them: *"Tata wesu leteni umunani kuno!"* ("For goodness sake! Please don't waste that tasty meat, bring it here!") He then took over the operations and instructed the boys to wash the dead hare thoroughly. He passed on the task of cooking it to one of his daughters-in-law. Later, the daughter-in-law graciously and respectfully served her father-in-law the midday meal consisting of tasty hare meat and seasoned vegetables, probably rape or sage, with nicely prepared *nshima,* a traditional Zambian meal made from thickened porridge (dough) of maize or cassava or rice flour.

Oh dear, by the time my baby sister had finished narrating this story to me, I was busy guessing who this daughter-in-law might have been and whether I myself had ever eaten any food cooked in her house when I was a child, as she may have used the same saucepans for cooking Grandad's dead hare! Anyway, we laughed our heads off and we both agreed that we were blessed to have had such a wonderful, crazy and entertaining grandfather who left us with so many unforgettable memories that we will keep on talking about him forever.

The Strange Diet of Snakes and Crocodiles in the Zambezi River

One of my good friends in England is married to a man who grew up along the Zambezi River in the North Western Province of Zambia. Mr Keith Katalayi Junior became a good source of information during my research for this book when

I was looking for reports of near mishaps or attacks on people by big snakes or crocodiles along the Zambezi River.

He started his stories by enlightening me on the history of Chitokoloki Mission in what was then Northern Rhodesia. This mission station was founded in 1807 by missionaries from Scotland, Ireland, New Zealand, Australia and England. The settlement was headed by Mr George Sucklene who belonged to a Christian faith, by then known as the Christian Mission in Many Lands.

Mr Katalayi told me that Chitokoloki Mission, which was built along the Zambezi River in the North Western Province, attracted many people to the educational facilities provided there by the CMML missionaries who, as well as a mission school, provided teacher training and a nursing school. He said there were also people who came looking for paid manual jobs.

Mr Katalayi reported that, as a young boy, he heard of and witnessed many incidents where people had lost their lives or just escaped attack by crocodiles and hippos on the reptile-infested Zambezi River. There were also reports of people being attacked by large, deadly snakes on the river banks or while they were working in nearby corn and rice fields.

He narrated a story where a family went out fishing one evening along the Zambezi River in their home-made canoe. A hippo saw them and emerged from the water and grabbed the front of the canoe, cutting it in half and dragging down whatever was alive and moving. Mr Katalayi explained that a hippo lives on grass and leaves; therefore, it does not eat fresh meat. He said the hippo's aim is to cut in half anything it perceives as a threat and thereafter leave it to its peril. Oh dear, can you imagine coming across a human being cut into two halves – a very scary prospect!

In another story, Mr Katalayi narrated an incident where his late mother was going to harvest her crop in a faraway rice field. She was accompanied by her favourite dog, which was running in front of her as they walked through the bushy fields. All of a sudden she heard the dog give a big yelp as it struggled with a python which was swallowing it alive. Keith's mother was unable to help the dog, but the python became immobile and numb after its large lunch, so she managed to escape and run away to call for help. Her husband came along and shot the python dead. When they cut open the snake's stomach, they found among other things, undigested stones, the remains of a hare, and the poor dog's carcass.

There were other incidents where villagers even found knives, swords and beads in the stomachs of dead crocodiles, as well as the bones of other animals. A woman had been drawing water from the Zambezi River when she noticed a crocodile swimming towards her. The woman's quick thinking saved her life. On seeing the crocodile, she quickly tilted the calabash she had been filling with water into the crocodile's pathway, which blocked its view of her and it only managed to grab the woman's knee. The clever woman pulled away and limped out of the water screaming and shouting for help. Mr Katalayi said the woman's cries were heard by schoolchildren who were paddling in a shallow pool near the riverbank with their teachers. They alerted older men from the village who ran to the woman's aid. Keith's father, who was a hunter, took his gun and eventually killed the crocodile. When they cut open the crocodile's stomach, they found inside it animal horns, a sword and a lot of women's beads.

Fortunately, there were newspaper reporters from *Nshila* newspaper in the area who visited the scene and publicised the story. Afterwards, porters took pictures of Mr Katalayi Senior posing with his gun placed on the massive crocodile's dead body. Keith's father became an instant hero and became highly respected in his village and beyond, where he was referred to as the Special Chief Hunter.

Young Mr Katalayi explained that finding beads in crocodile stomachs usually confirmed that a female villager had been killed and eaten by the reptile in question. The wearing of beads around the waist and neck is an old cultural and traditional practice for women in most African countries. Swallowed items like metal, bones and beads can remain in the reptile's stomach for many years after the flesh from a swallowed animal or person has been digested.

An important point was raised by Keith regarding the deadly bile found in the crocodiles' stomachs. He said that his father used to burn the stomach and then bury it in a deep hole, as evil men in his village were inclined to use it to create a deadly poisonous cocktail to inflict on fellow unsuspecting villagers.

I have been told unconfirmed stories of villagers finding a hand with a wristwatch still wrapped around it in a dead crocodile's stomach. I have also been told of a certain stretch of the Zambezi River where there is a type of fish that swallows diamonds. When fishermen gut the fish, they find diamonds still intact in the intestines. Probably the fish accidentally swallow diamonds just as they swallow any other stones when looking for food on the river bed. I am sure a lot of fishing goes on in the area, as who wouldn't like to catch a fish which had swallowed ounces of diamonds? You could rightly call them fishy diamonds or smelly diamonds!

The Protruding Chicken Neck in the Casserole

As though eating a dead hare from a snake's stomach was not enough, my baby sister narrated another story where she and Grandad were at home alone while Grandma had gone out on various errands.

My sister remembers Grandad saying, "*Mpundu mukolwe twipike umunani washupa pa ng'anda.*" He asked her to chase and catch the biggest cockerel, as it appeared there wasn't enough meat in the house. My sister said that she summoned other children to join her in the chase and, after a long, tiresome run around the compound, the biggest cockerel was apprehended. Mpundu, which was my sister's birth name, brought the frightened chicken to Grandad, who then laid the twitching, protesting creature across a large flat stone. Holding the chicken firmly down, he took another sharp flattened stone and used it as an axe to cut off the chicken's head.

As the chicken's head came off, says my sister who was standing nearby, the headless body went into vigorous spasms which frightened her badly. Grandad went into action: he dipped the chicken carcass into boiling water (for ease of removing the feathers) then plucked it and cleaned it, and instructed Mpundu to put it into a saucepan and boil it over the specially made oven fire. To my sister's surprise, each time she lifted the lid to check on the water level in the pot, the chicken's neck would shoot out as if it was still alive. My sister became petrified and ran away screaming. Grandad thought it was all very funny!

As an adult, my sister can see the funny side now. In fits of laughter, she concluded her story by saying that, on that evening, she refused to indulge in the meal of chicken, vegetables and *nshima* prepared by Grandma. Furthermore, she stopped eating chicken meat altogether after that frightening episode of seeing a dead chicken poke its neck out of a boiling saucepan.

My sister and I both agreed that those were tough years, and that we had witnessed some happenings that might have come out of a horror film. We reminded ourselves and thanked the Lord Almighty that nowadays we can buy chicken products already processed and wrapped, and all we need to do is simply add a few seasoning ingredients and cook them in the oven.

For these stories, I am thankful to my baby sister, my best friend. Despite the great distance between us, we laugh and chat on the phone like any two sisters sitting in one room, in the same house, in the same country, and yet we are thousands of miles apart – one in England and the other in Zambia.

We both feel blessed to have known and lived with our grandad whom we adored, and appreciate him for sharing with us his priceless life stories. In doing so, he has implanted in our memories a rich, exciting world history which will be passed on from one generation to another.

CHAPTER TWELVE

GRANDAD'S HILARIOUS STORIES

G randad Mulutula, a man of many talents: Dr David Livingstone's pallbearer, village headman, village judge, traditional healer, the champion at inheriting deceased relatives' wives, the proud husband, father, stepfather, grandfather, uncle and brother...

Among the many fascinating abilities of my grandad, I loved him most for his storytelling sessions which would begin after the evening meal and would continue until late into the night when he would abruptly stop telling the story and announce in his deep soft voice, *"Tata wesu bwaila, and kalaleni mailo mukaya ku sukulu!"* ("For goodness' sake, it is getting late, go to sleep, you have to go to school tomorrow morning.") Then, holding each other's hands, my cousins and I would stand up sleepily and go to our allocated sleeping rooms in the round passage.

As mentioned earlier, Grandad's house was a large round house made of burnt bricks. It had a passage around the outside which was divided into sections. The Far East wing was my grandparents' sleeping quarters or bedroom which accommodated a good-sized bed; otherwise it was full of large iron trunks, as well as ordinary travelling suitcases. I was one of the few children allowed to enter our grandparents' portion of the house. On rare occasions and when Grandad was away on his many tours and travels, Grandma used to invite me to sleep in their bedroom. The middle part of the passage was the girls' sleeping quarters, while the far north or west wing was the section allocated to my male cousins. The large central room was the oval sitting room where adults sat when drinking and eating, and sometimes it was used as a courtroom when Grandad convened any court hearings.

Apart from the Great Epic Journey which recounts his part in bringing Dr David Livingstone's body back to England, Grandad told us other stories about his service to his colonial masters. One of our favourites was the one about the magical talking invoice notes, received from the colonial administrators at the Fort Jameson depot where servants used to go and collect salt consignments to be delivered to their colonial master based inland.

Northern Rhodesia, (or Zambia as it's now known), being a landlocked country, depended on dispatching and receiving goods and provisions through ports such as Mpulungu Port near Abercorn, (now renamed Mbala), a small town on the shores of Lake Mpulungu at the northernmost point of the country. This lake connected Northern Rhodesia to East African countries. From there, trade was carried on across the Indian Ocean to other continents.

The Magical Talking Invoice Note

Grandad worked for white people based in the Central and Northern Provinces of Zambia, whose main cargo route was via what is now Mbala. Periodically, porters or servants were dispatched to Mbala to take any merchandise to be shipped to East Africa and other far-off places. On their return journey, they brought goods arriving from East Africa and abroad. Possibly the most important merchandise was unprocessed salt. Colonial administrators at Mpulungu would issue an invoice to their inland counterparts, indicating the amount of salt they had handed over to the porters.

However, disgruntled porters came up with a trick of removing some of the salt from the bags and then carefully sealing them up again before continuing on their journey back to their unsuspecting masters. However, on arrival, the weight indicated on the written invoice would not match the weight of the consignment at hand. The unsuspecting inland masters could only wonder if the discrepancy was an error made by the administrators at the Mbala depot, as their trusted porters would swear upon their children's lives that they knew nothing about the disappearance of such large quantities of salt from the consignment they were given at the Mbala dispatch depot.

The first time it happened, the colonial master did not take much notice as he thought the error must have been a simple mistake at Mbala depot.

However, the cunning porters believed the only way their master could know that some salt had been removed from the sealed bags was by receiving a spoken message from the invoice itself, that had witnessed the theft. They conspired and agreed that next time round, the porter keeping the invoice should go and hide behind the anthill with the invoice in his pocket while they removed some salt from the sealed bags. In Zambia, there are huge anthills, the likes of which you will not see in the UK; they can be as tall as a house, and easily big enough to hide behind. They foolishly thought such a plan would prevent the note from seeing them in action, hence would no one would witness the theft in progress and would not be able to report it to the master on their arrival.

Once again on their second trip, the porters presented the merchandise they had collected from Mbala, which again weighed less than the amount indicated on the invoice. This time the colonial master became suspicious and threatened to flog the porters and dock their pay for stealing the salt. Then the cowardly porter who was asked to hide behind the anthill with the note became angry as he felt he was unfairly implicated in the theft. He decided to confess and report the other porters' criminal activities to the master.

So he went to the master and explained that he was an innocent person who had been persuaded to hide with the invoice in his pocket as the other porters did not want the invoice note to witness the theft of salt in progress. The white master could not believe his porters' naïve and superstitious mentality. He therefore called the porters and confronted them with what he had been told. They confessed to committing the offence but told the white man that the amount he paid them was not enough to sustain them and their families, which was why they stole salt to sell to subsidise their meagre wages.

The good, kind master understood their desperation and felt sorry for them. He nonetheless docked their pay, and only reinstated them on condition that the porters agreed to spend their spare time learning Bible verses. He also imparted to them the essence of the Ten Commandments which the master insisted his porters should follow at all times; reminding them to bear in their minds that stealing from their own master is a sin. He read to them one of the Ten Commandments which says, 'Thou shalt not steal'.

Laughing and jokingly urging us not to steal from our parents or teachers, Grandad would conclude his story by praising his kind and Godly-hearted colonial master who had agreed that the porters' wages should be increased after the salt-stealing incident. He told us there was a good outcome to the story as they all started going for a few hours' of basic Bible study and began to attend church, obediently upholding the teachings and doctrines of the Ten Commandments thereafter.

The Grounded Witches

Sometimes Grandad's stories were scary and spine-tingling for us children, some as young as five years old. However, we all loved the storytelling sessions and there would be a big group of children of different ages sitting around the fire while Grandad sat on his high stool, delivering his stories, one after another, in his deep, softly-spoken velvet voice.

Grandad would finish his story and shift a little on his stool, staring round at our faces. Then he would give a big chuckle to the delight of the attentive, mesmerised grandchildren. Sometimes after Grandad had sent us to bed, it was difficult for us children to go to sleep as we were scared and frightened of encountering the witches whom Grandad had grounded when they had tried to trespass into his territory.

There were nights when we would huddle together, clinging to each other for dear life on our sleeping mattresses, after hearing noises from growling thunderstorms or howling hyenas which we would mistake for witches.

It all started with all my boy cousins telling Grandad that they had seen for themselves grounded witches crawling naked around the village at dawn. The boys would become hysterical and start shouting about how many they had seen, and Grandad would enthusiastically fall in with their stories and ask open questions like, "Who did you see? That one with short grey hair was the tenth witch I grounded." Then another cousin would shout loudly that he had seen a naked man running into the bush early one morning but hadn't told anybody, and Grandad would laugh and say, "Oh, yes. That one – he was a foreigner and new to this area. I had to release him because he pleaded with me and said he had just got married to a widow and she would divorce him if she heard he went around bewitching people in surrounding villages." Such stories of seeing grounded witches would go on and on. I would sit there wondering how Grandad did it, at the same time telling myself that I would like to see one in the flesh for myself.

I was always a heavy sleeper which meant I used to wake up late, but one morning I decided to get up early so I might also see some grounded witches. On this day, I jumped up at the first light of the rising sun. I dashed outside Grandad's house, hoping to see crawling figures – alas, all I saw were dogs and cats fighting over food, leftovers thrown out by housewives cleaning their cooking utensils while sitting in rays of the rising sun.

Eventually, I gathered my courage and asked Grandma about the grounded witches who had trespassed into our village. Her first reaction was of horror and disappointment, and she asked me where I had heard such things. I told her that Grandad and my boy cousins had seen naked crawling men and women who had been grounded by Grandad at dawn. Grandma's face dropped and she was momentarily lost for words. She gathered me up into her arms and, while stroking my hair, said almost in a whisper, "Grandad is good at telling stories," but under her breath she mouthed scornfully, "*Ubufi,*

ubufi," ("lies, lies"). Then, realising what she had said, she pulled me closer and said, "Listen to me very clearly, little one, do not take everything Grandad says as the whole truth. Some of them are simply stories, but you should only listen and obey his instructions." As an afterthought she said, "Little one, young girls are not supposed to see naked old men running into the bush." And then she let go of me. I just stood motionless, not knowing what to do or say. But eventually and unexpectedly, I looked up at her and said, "Yes Grandma." At that time, I didn't know if I was replying to her earlier sceptical sentiments or if I was agreeing with her words of warning. But then I realised that I felt happier and reassured by knowing that I was a little girl and that was why I did not see naked grounded witches. Having said that, I was the first in the queue to go and sit down near the fire to listen to Grandad's evening stories.

In hindsight, Grandma must have had a strong word with Grandad about the kind of stories he told us children because the type of stories suddenly changed from scary witchdoctor stories to more relevant and factual stories, full of wisdom, and mostly based on our cultural traditions, values and beliefs.

The Demented Wanderers

Writing about Grandad's downed witches today, I cannot help feeling sorry for those poor souls. Since those days, I have become a trained social worker and I am a dementia friend, so bells started ringing from the time I started writing about the downed witches who trespassed into Katobole village. The most probable explanation for accounts of crawling naked men and women is probably that these were demented elderly people from neighbouring villages who had lost their way while wandering in their dementia trances and trying to find their way back home.

A wandering dementia sufferer would not even remember her or his name and, worse still, would not know where they came from; they would be confused and disorientated in time and place. These poor souls in a village environment would probably go to sleep undressed and unsupervised, then wake up at dawn confused and disoriented and start wandering away from home. Even these days in the UK where I live now, we have wanderers who are found in very dangerous places, like walking by the motorway or by river banks or canals at odd times. These days, and in Western societies, people are more aware of dementia and its associated symptoms such as hallucinations, incoherent speech and unkempt appearances, therefore in cases where someone is found or seen wandering in inappropriate circumstances, the police or other emergency care services can be alerted.

The Disgruntled Killer Prince

With his new style of story-telling, Grandad would start another tale by saying:

"Once upon a time, there was this big, big kingdom which was so big that the king decided to give part of it to his youngest son. The youngest prince therefore became the ruler of a large portion of his father's kingdom. However, as the king had married many wives, and had several other children, his gift to the youngest prince brought jealousy and hatred which resulted in fighting within the royal family. In frustration and anger, the young prince suspected that his father's elders had plotted against him and that they were the ones inciting other members of the royal family to rise against him. The young prince therefore decided to kill and eliminate all the old folks above a certain age in the kingdom, including his own father. Within a short period, all the old people were dead and the kingdom was soon inhabited just by vibrant young men and women."

Grandad would continue: "Unknown to the forceful, menacing young prince and his youthful subjects, one old man had managed to escape and hide from being kidnapped and killed by the prince's soldiers. The old man had taken refuge in a nearby thicket where he survived by drinking rainwater and feeding on wild fruits. He also killed small animals which he cooked on an open fire at night. The old man had also made himself a sleeping canvas high up in the branches of a big strong mukwa tree. By living such an isolated and secluded life, he managed to conceal his existence.

"At first, everybody led a jubilant, vibrant life, full of new ideas for their everlasting harmonious kingdom. Then an unexpected omen struck. The entire kingdom was overwhelmed by the arrival of massive house rats which fed on people's flesh from their feet at night. The rats would sneak into the people's sleeping mats at night and bite or nip at their toes, their feet, their faces or eyes and literally suck human blood from their body parts."

At this point, we children listening to the story would hold onto each other as though checking we were not being bitten by rats as we sat listening to Grandad's stories. Sensing our agitation, Grandad would say, "By the way, the rats were so clever, they could bite and then blow cold air on the bites to dampen the pain, so sleeping people did not know they were being bitten or eaten by the rats until they woke up the following morning and found gaping wounds on their feet. And some could feel blood oozing from their bitten eyelids and lips."

Grandad would then pause, look round to ensure that nobody had dozed off and then he would continue in a much more sombre voice: "As though the arrival of rats was not enough trouble for the prince and his young subjects, swarms of snakes descended on the kingdom coming to feed on the rats!"

Yankee! All of us children would jump up or cling to each other and the expressionless Grandad would continue while rolling his eyes: "While rats only bit and sucked human blood, the snakes were lethal and came with a vengeance as their poisonous bites killed people."

"Ooooh!" we would all moan.

Then Grandad would pause again and resume the story: "On several occasions, the poisonous snakes swallowed human babies alive." We would recoil in fear as we visualised a snake swallowing a live baby. We would wait nervously for the next phase of the story and check to ensure there were no snakes sneaking under our folded legs. Grandad would continue:

"One day, a big snake was hiding in a woman's hut, watching her as she breastfed her baby. He said the snake became overwhelmed by the smell of baby milk and slithered out of its hiding place, making for the woman's baby. But the brave woman acted quickly and threw the baby into the air. The baby landed on the other side of the hut. The frustrated snake then started coiling itself around the body of the woman, squeezing every bone in her body. The woman started screaming for help."

At this point, Grandad would purposely pause, and we would all start asking, "So what happened to this woman?" Then, raising his voice, Grandad would say, "When the young inhabitants arrived to help the woman and saw a big snake wrapped around her body, they went wild and ran away in different directions!"

We would all wriggle our tiny bodies as though the snake was wrapping itself around us and go, "Ooooh, whoops!" and some children would stand up, almost in tears as the pictures in their imagination became too much to take in while seated. Then raising his hands in the air and dropping them slowly, Grandad would whisper and say, "Then from nowhere, the old man who had been hiding in the thicket heard the commotion and came running. Before anybody even thought about why an old man should be alive among them, he quickly looked for a live rat, which he let loose into the woman's hut where the snake could see it. As the rat scrambled to run away on the smeared hut floor, the snake saw it and unwrapped itself from the woman's body, setting her free and pouncing upon the rat. The onlookers started cheering and clapping their hands. The old man tenderly lifted up the frightened woman whose first instinct was to crawl to her baby who was still lying where she had thrown him, unscathed and unaware of the fate he had escaped in his mother's hut."

Grandad would then conclude his story by saying that the young prince spared the old man's life and congratulated him for executing the rescue mission so precisely. The prince showed his gratitude by awarding the old man a piece of land where he built him a house and assured him that he would allow old folks to live in his kingdom and he brought some lucky ones from his old father's kingdom to live together with the young ones.

Then Grandad would give us a lecture about the importance of respecting and listening to old folks' wisdom which they had gained through their lifelong experiences.

The Lazy Scarred Boy
with a Dribbling Chin

Grandad would then shift on his stool, pick up a long stick and poke it into the burning fire. Bright sparks would fly into the sky like fireworks!

Then he would say to us amongst the excited laughter at the sparkling fireworks, "Take it from me, this story I am going to tell you next is a true story." We all answered at once, "Yes Grandad! Tell us now please, please!" Then he would begin:

"Once upon a time, there was a lazy, greedy boy who always refused to go out hunting or fishing with his father or any other older men in the village. This boy preferred to stay at home and watch his mother prepare delicious family meals. Unknown to his mother, the son used to steal and eat large portions of cooked food before it was served to other members of the family, including his obnoxious father who continually beat up his wife for serving him small portions of food, some without his favourite and sacred pieces of meat."

In Grandad's era, chicken soup would be served with chicken legs and gizzards, a special delicacy. A gizzard is served only to a husband or man of the house as a sign of respect. Any meal served without meat could be declined and the woman serving such a dish could be beaten up and eventually divorced by her enraged husband.

It was therefore no surprise that the lazy boy's obnoxious father kept beating up his wife for serving lacklustre meals without the special delicacies which should have been preserved for him. Grandad continued and said that for a long time, the woman endured a life of beatings and incessant insults, together with the man's threats of divorcing her.

However, one day, the woman's husband killed a wild pig and requested his wife prepare the pig's tail mixed with bean soup, which apparently was his favourite meal. The woman hastily prepared the requested dish and, as she had past concerns about cooked food disappearing in the house, she decided to hide the clay pot containing the pig's tail and bean soup on top of a high, improvised kitchen cupboard. The woman then left the house to go and fetch water from the stream for her husband's bath.

In the meantime, the lazy boy who was hiding in his improvised hut, swallowing buckets of saliva on smelling the delicious soup his mother was cooking, could not even wait for his mother's shadow to disappear before he dived into the tiny kitchen, rummaging through the cooking pots, looking for the one containing the tasty smelling soup.

Grandad would then lower his voice and say, "As fate had it, that the clay pot containing the soup was still sizzling hot from its long time cooking. However, the boy spotted the pot high on the cupboard shelf and, with his mouth wide open, the lurking, lousy lout tilted the hot pot towards himself." Grandad would exclaim and describe the disastrous catastrophe that followed, as the boiling soup poured over his open mouth, severely burning his lips, tongue, throat, chin, neck and chest.

At this point, we children would raise our hands and cover our mouths in horror as though to avoid hot soup pouring into our own mouths. Then Grandad would continue with his story and add a funny quip like, "By the way, it was also strongly rumoured that the boy's frontals got burnt as well." Then we would all stand up and nervously clutch our frontals as though to ensure that ours were safe and untouched. One by one we would ask Grandad why the boy's frontals were also burnt. "God forgive us, that foolish lazy boy slept all the time and when he dived into the kitchen, he had no clothes on!"

Amid nervous laughter, some of the older ones wanted to know exactly what else was burnt. Grandad would cough and exaggerate some kind of disgust and continue with his story.

He went on to say that by the time the boy's mother heard his screams and rushed back to the house, she found him lying on the floor, bent double in pain. There were pieces of the broken clay pot strewn all over the floor and hot steam oozing from pieces of pig's tail and the bean soup soaking into the debris on the kitchen floor.

Grandad finished narrating his story by emphasising that the boy was scarred for life. Strings of burnt skin from his lips adhered to burnt skin on his neck, which in turn got connected to the burnt skin on his chest. In the end, the lousy lad sustained a permanent disability with badly scarred and stretched skin connecting his lips, chin, neck and chest; hence he had a permanently open mouth which dribbled continuously.

We children sat there looking at each other wide-eyed, imagining this lazy boy with an open mouth, with scarred burnt skin. Covering our lips, neck and chest protectively with our arms, we would then mumble, "Ugh, that is not very nice, Grandad."

Finally, before retiring to bed, our satisfied grandfather would give us a lecture about the evils of being greedy and lazy, but most of all he would emphasise the disastrous consequences of stealing from our own parents. He would then refer us to one of the Ten Commandments in the Bible: Thou shalt not steal.

The Curse of an Evil Foreign Daughter-in-Law

Another story was about a horrible evil woman who married into a noble family and then disrupted and dismantled the peace and tranquillity that the family had enjoyed before her arrival.

Grandad would once more assure us that the tale he was about to tell was a true story and all of us would just sit there waiting to hear this new story. If anyone coughed the rest of us would go, "Ooooh? Nooo! Nooo! Stop coughing, we want to hear Grandad's story!"

Then Grandad would adjust himself on the stool and begin:

"Once upon a time, there was a young man whose father was a very rich and important man in the village. Everybody in the village wondered about his prolonged bachelorhood as the young man did not take any interest in local girls. He was a very generous and kind person who cared about and respected every family member in his father's entire household. Hence his father's subjects saw him as a leader-in-waiting and were therefore anxious to marry their daughters to him.

"Surprisingly, the young man went on an unannounced tour and was absent from the village for many weeks. When he returned he brought with him a very beautiful woman who he said had come from a faraway land across many lakes and rivers. He announced that he had married her.

"The proud young man's father hastily arranged for a week-long wedding celebration to welcome the new bride to his village. It was a time of joy and merriment and the villagers did their best to show their happiness at having their odd bachelor boy get hitched to a beautiful foreign woman. The carnival, or wedding party, lasted a week, during which the bride and groom were showered with gifts and presents of all kinds, such as cloth, money, cattle, gold and beads.

"Within a short time," continued Grandad, "the new bride's true colours started to surface. She started restricting the number of people her husband should help or support. She prevented other family members from having access to her husband. As if that wasn't enough, she disrespected her in-laws to the extent that other daughters-in-law had to take over the responsibility of providing care for the elderly parents. In most African traditional customs, the wife of the youngest son should look after and care for her husband's parents. She also started requesting more and more servants to carry out chores and errands, which were normally executed by the housewives. In doing so, her husband's coffers started to rapidly dwindle to the extent that his father noticed and took steps to put a stop to his son's spending spree. Unfortunately, her father-in-law's threats to dishonour his son angered the foreign wife.

"She eventually became so powerful that she undermined her husband's powers, inciting him to carry out certain actions which were not well received by her in-laws. Hence the father-in-law became depressed and bitter as he tried hopelessly to correct the situation and restore harmony in his fragmented family. In the end there was an open rift between father and son which led to the rich man's mysterious death. Everyone in the village suspected that the father-in-law had been poisoned by his evil daughter-in-law who, on the very rare occasion, had offered to prepare a meal for him. After consuming the meal, the father-in-law became unwell and started vomiting blood and had such bad diarrhoea that he was dead within hours of his meal. Everybody in the village wanted to know whether the old man had died of food poisoning or a natural death. However, the evil wife and her husband were untouchable and nobody could question her on how the food she served her father-in-law had been prepared.

"However, after a very dramatic period of mourning, the events which followed included the evil woman's husband taking over all of his father's wealth. On the instructions of the wife, the son cut off his mother and other brothers and sisters from the dead man's estate. The evil daughter-in-law then brought her immediate family to come and live with her to lead a life of luxury while the husband's family began to live in dire poverty. They begged for food and slept rough as they had been chased from their own houses by the evil woman and her husband in order to leave living quarters for the woman's family. Very soon, the whole village was seized with anger."

At this point in the story, Grandad would stretch himself and then continue: "One day, the evil woman woke up from her sleep and discovered that her entire body was covered in weeping boils, the size of my thumbnail. They had even grown on her lips, her eyes, her eyelids and ears, her nose, her forehead and her hands and legs. She panicked and woke her husband and her entire family, showing them how she had been transformed into an alien. Nobody came near her as they feared her weeping boils could be contagious. She started screaming and demanded to be taken to a medicine man who could cure her of the illness. Her husband and her family took her from one medicine man to another until they reached a traditional fortune-teller who was also a healer. He told her that she had been cursed by her dead father-in-law whom she had purposely poisoned and that the boils were there to stay as punishment for ill-treating and dragging a respectable family into disarray and misery. However, the traditional healer said he could bring her misery to an end on the condition that she obeyed his instructions which had been given to him as prophecy from high up in heaven."

Grandad went on to explain what she had to do. First of all, the evil woman had to find white chickens or doves which she was supposed to deliver personally to every individual she had insulted or treated badly. Secondly, the evil woman should give back all her wealth, including that of her husband, to the dead man's family. And thirdly, she should tell all her relatives to leave the village and let the original inhabitants come back to their houses. The woman eagerly agreed to follow the instructions as she was anxious to get healed of the watery, weeping boils.

The miserable boil-infected woman started by asking her relatives to leave her husband's village. Then she handed over to her mother-in-law and all her husband's immediate family the wealth she and her husband had amassed from the dead man. Then she proceeded to buy white chickens and doves which she was expected to deliver to the people she had offended, and she apologised. She managed to speak to and seek forgiveness from a few of her husband's relatives and then she went to face her mother-in-law whom she had treated so badly earlier. The mother-in-law, who was a very kind and religious woman, accepted the woman's dove and apology but she said to her, "My dear child, no matter how many people you apologise to, you have killed my husband through greed and you therefore have blood on your hands. He is not here to listen to or accept your apology, therefore you will remain with your watery, weeping boils until you meet him in heaven and apologise to him personally."

The evil woman threw herself on the ground and started weeping and screaming, asking for forgiveness from the dead man. Her husband eventually heard her screams and came over, picked her up and asked her to leave his house and village. Weeping and shaking badly himself, he knelt down and profusely apologised to his mother for what the evil woman had incited him to do to her and his entire family. He said he was divorcing her and would take up his father's reins to look after the family and the village and bring back the harmony they had always enjoyed.

Grandad Would then Say, "The End!"

We would all exclaim, "Whaaoo!" And then we would all ask at once, "What happened to the evil woman? Where did she go?"

Then Grandad would look around with a broad smile on his face as though he was not listening to our anxious questions and say, "Probably she died." And before anybody could ask how she died, how she was buried or whether her husband attended the funeral, Grandad would start giving us a lecture on how important it is to respect in-laws, people in authority, teachers and ordinary elders in the community. He would also lecture us on the evils of greediness and that we should learn to share things from an early age. He would say, "Don't claim ownership of anything which does not belong to you." And to round it all off Grandad would recite his favourite saying:

"If you live life recklessly like lightening, you will crash like thunder."

CHAPTER THIRTEEN

SANDAUNI – DANCING FROM SUNRISE TILL DAWN

When I was about five years old, my Uncle Charlie, Granddad's nephew, had just arrived in Katobole village from the Nchanga copper mines at Chingola on the Copperbelt where he worked as a miner. He had come to arrange our annual Sandauni event.

He was a town boy and, as such, he dressed and spoke differently from us at Katobole Village. Grandma told me he had stopped eating *nshima*, Zambia's staple dish made from corn or cassava flour. It is a staple food in most African countries. She went on to explain that Uncle Charlie had been complaining that *nshima* was too traditional and too African, so now he preferred to eat Irish potatoes or rice with fish or meat, chicken and vegetables. I was surprised and could not comprehend what Grandma was telling me. It was like an Englishman saying he no longer eats fish and chips, just because he now works in China. I could not sleep properly that night as I thought about how cheeky Uncle Charlie had become. Who did he think he was? In my childish mind I thought that everyone in the world ate *nshima.* I thought the only difference was that white people ate softer *nshima* because they had delicate white bodies which could not digest hard *nshima.*

To help out with the Sandauni preparations, Charlie put the young men and teenage boys in the village to work. He wrote out advertisements and posters on sheets of paper and told them to stick them up on trees all over the village and in many other surrounding villages, including those across the Itandashi River, which geographically marks the Northern and Luapula Provinces of North East Zambia. Katobole village is in the Luwingu District of the Northern Province while the villages across the river are part of Luapula Province. The boundary meant nothing really; we had relatives across the river and people used to fish together in the Itandashi River without taking note of who belonged to which province – they are the same people but reported to different administrative offices. However, to give credit to Uncle Charlie, his method of advertising the Sandauni event was a big hit and people talked about it across the borders for weeks.

In the second phase of preparation for Sandauni, Uncle Charlie mobilised the boys and turned his attention to erecting an enclosure the size of a football pitch on the outskirts of the village. He then advertised for stand holders inside the enclosure for sales of food, fruit, drinks, and home-brewed and bottled beer. Finally, Uncle Charlie hired a battery-run gramophone for playing records. He also approached individual musicians and drummers to perform live music on the day. The preparations took up to two weeks.

On the appointed Sandauni day, the atmosphere at Katobole village became electric. Mothers bathed and dressed their younger children early. Wives and engaged girls fetched and boiled water for their partners' hot baths. Teenage boys and girls started marching to Itandashi River for their early swims in readiness for the partying ahead of them. Towards midday, Uncle Charlie and another town acquaintance dressed up and took their dignified places at the Sandauni enclosure's gate. Whoever passed through the gate had to pay an agreed fee.

Then the party-goers started pouring in, all dressed to impress. Young men and teenage boys wore their best attire, complete with polished shoes. The young women and teenage girls added flavour to the event with their displays of colourful African outfits and various western suits, dresses, skirts and floral tops. Some wore hats to complement their outfits and matched them with high-heeled shoes. What a combination of spectacle and beauty! Those trying to enter the enclosure roughly dressed were quickly escorted out by Uncle Charlie and his town-dweller friend. It was like the movies. Katobole village was swamped by nicely dressed people and the atmosphere changed into a carnival mood. The enclosure started filling up and the music from the gramophone started bellowing enticing music which could be heard miles and miles away. Sellers were busy selling their commodities while other participants started dancing to the beautiful, inviting and romantic melodies.

Then the Master of Ceremonies blew a whistle and called for everybody's attention. He began to announce the pledges received from suitors wanting to dance with specifically chosen ladies who had already caught their eyes. Ooooh, ooooh, there we go, one suitor pledges for a particular lady and then he is outdone by another who pledges a higher stake, and so the bidding continues until the highest unchallenged one is announced. The proud bidder then steps out, and like a peacock leads his chosen partner to the dancefloor. It was a magical moment; the dancefloor was quickly transformed into a wonderful sea of total beauty and splendour.

Those girls could dance as well as any professional dancers. The ladies graced the dance floor with their beauty and dance skills and the manner in which they light-footedly wiggled their hips to any danceable tune was purely electric. Every stallion in the enclosure wanted to hold them and dance with them, no matter how much they had to pledge to beat the other punters. Money was flying about and the Master of Ceremonies was drumming up the excitement with his tantalising announcements: *"Haaah, haaah, mwashala mwashala yama – oooh, oooh, moneni abakashana ubusuma, yangu tabakwata amafupa mumisana yabo,"* which means something like, "Haaah, haaah, you can't look at these beautiful women with flexible, well-shaped waists."

After such utterances, the Master of Ceremonies jumped up in the air and landed on one foot and twisted as if he had no bones in his body – all this to the delight of the punters who started pledging even larger sums of money, having loosened up from having had one or two alcoholic drinks. By now the pledges were being collected in sackfuls. Who would have guessed that these were villagers engaged in poorly-paid small-scale jobs in manganese ore extraction which was processed at a battery factory at Mansa and some sent far afield by both local and foreign companies.

The bidding and the dancing reached its climax and some of the couples became inseparable. Some of the punters began to get disgruntled at the men who would not let go of the most beautiful and skilled dancers, despite their higher pledges, and started fuming and throwing insults at them. The Master of Ceremonies was accused of favouritism and got an earful of insults.

Suddenly the dancefloor was invaded by aggressive younger men who could not resist their testosterone urges and started pulling dancing girls away from their partners. Chaos! Chaos! Women were being pulled first one way, then the other in the midst of very strong words from both. Ooooh, ooooh, my Uncle Charlie and his friend had to get busy separating the sex-starved angry young men. The Master of Ceremonies started to be accused of cheating them out of their right to claim the dancers, despite having paid their higher pledges.

Out of the blue, a nephew of my Grandad Mulutula emerged from a dark corner where he had been drinking bottled beer. Isake Chamutobo was known as the village deviant, a villain and a jailbird. He had noticed the confusion unfolding and decided to take advantage of the situation to promote his own selection of white music.

Chamutobo portrayed himself as a town-educated fellow and did things differently from the villagers. He spouted off about things he had learnt from various prisons where he had spent most of his life – he knew things about the world outside of Africa, like the Korean and Vietnam wars. He also knew the names of the world's greatest boxers or fighters like Cassius Clay, George Foreman and Sugar Ray Robinson. Each time he returned from his long-term prison sentences, he would rename all the village boys with names of boxers, footballers and even world presidents. The village boys would be so proud of their new names that some kept them for life. Chamutobo therefore enjoyed the star treatment he got at Katobole village for being so knowledgeable, and children worshipped him, oblivious of the fact that he was a hardcore criminal. Chamutobo instructed us children that we should address him as Army Captain or Lieutenant John Spoon.

Sometimes children ignored their parents' warnings against getting close to Chamutobo. Girls were warned by their mothers never to go near. Grandma severely warned me not to listen to his fabricated stories, but the attraction was so strong that sometimes I disobeyed her and escaped with my male cousins to listen to Chamutobo's stories, which were both interesting and fascinating. He would sit there surrounded by thirty to fifty youngsters, preaching to them about town life, and then later he would tell them to go and steal money and possessions from their own parents.

To adults, Chamutobo was a nuisance. Each time he was arrested in a faraway province, he would impersonate male Katobole villagers and give their names to the police. Katobole village was constantly invaded by menacing mobile police who came looking for an innocent villager whose name had been given by Chamutobo. Unlucky ones would be roughly thrown into police trucks until Grandad pleaded for them, explaining to police officers that they had arrested the wrong person as the culprit they were looking for was Chamutobo known by authorities as 'Mr John Spoon'. It took authorities a long time to learn that Chamutobo was the hardcore criminal and trickster who impersonated innocent law-abiding Katobole male villagers.

Coming back to the scenario in the Sandauni enclosure: Chamutobo left the riot in the enclosure, and appeared a few minutes later with a bundle of records securely held under his left arm. He strode straight up to the platform where the gramophone was playing and stopped the music. Instead, the voice of a Jim Reeves song blared out. The dancing couples looked at each other nervously and, holding hands, walked off until the entire dance floor was deserted. Chamutobo was dressed in a strange, badly fitting, unsuitable three-piece suit with a long black jacket on top, which must have been stolen from an unsuspecting, decent white gentleman because the suit even had sophisticated chains pinned to the front of the jacket. The trousers were too long for Chamutobo, who was a short, stout man, so he was almost tripping over them. Anyway, Chamutobo graced the empty floor, swinging from side to side, his hands spread high above his head. Every now and again, he tilted his head at an angle, as if whispering to, or kissing his imaginary ballroom dancing partner. Watching in amazement and totally embarrassed, everybody was saying, "*Iyeeee mayo*?" or "What is going on?"

In those days, the early to mid-sixties, showing affection in public was frowned upon and regarded as taboo. Hence Chamutobo's dancing antics sent shivers through the veins of the young traditionalists. Suddenly a voice announced loudly and clearly: "We do not want white man's music... eeeeh! We have paid to dance to rumba and jive music!"

Chamutobo abruptly stopped his swinging and charged in the direction of the tall, smartly dressed man who had just spoken. With his bloodshot eyes bulging out of his head, the furious Chamutobo tried to throw a punch and a header at the same time, but Uncle Charlie, who had sensed the mood change, was standing only inches away from the smart young man and leapt at Chamutobo, putting him in a headlock.

Uncle Charlie slightly loosened his hold and Chamutobo looked up at the tall man and started cursing him bitterly: "Do you know me, eeeh? Get out of my face! Ask the others, my name is Lieutenant John Spoon or Beula!" Still held tightly by my uncle, he continued ranting: "I will throw you up in the sky until your shadow turns a million times! Then your body will drop and crumble in a heap of ashes on the ground!" Then he would swing his head violently and say, "Oh yes, I will cut you down when I apply my calisthenics army training on you! I am Lieutenant Spoon who fought in both the Korean and the Vietnam wars!"

This only produced fits of laughter, especially from the women. The young men urged Uncle Charlie to throw Chamutobo out of the enclosure so the dancing could resume.

Uncle Charlie and his town friend dragged Chamutobo away and out of the enclosure and soon the rumba music started booming again and couples moved onto the dancefloor.

Things went on smoothly for a while until eeeeeeh! In strode Chamutobo to the Sandauni enclosure, this time dressed in a white doctor's coat, complete with a stethoscope hanging around his neck! Everyone in the enclosure laughed, "Whaaaah – what the hell is going on?" One of the young men, probably a bit drunk, shouted, "Where did you steal the doctor's coat and his stethoscope, Chamutobo? We know you are a thief; why don't you leave us alone?" Chamutobo looked right and left and then dashed in the direction of where the voice had come from. Uncle Charlie, who now had a strategic group of bouncers around him, once more leapt at Chamutobo. They were angry now, for spoiling their Sandauni celebrations and they tore off his white coat and stethoscope and dragged him away. This time they warned him that they would call the mobile police stationed nearby at the manganese ore depot to come and arrest him for being a nuisance at their party. Chamutobo, who knew he was wanted by the police, dead or alive, ran off and disappeared into thin air. Nobody heard from him again until a few years later when he was next released from prison.

The party resumed, and the dancing continued into the early hours. Children and decent married couples had long retired to bed, leaving the frisky young stallions and their fillies to dance the night away.

The following morning, Uncle Charlie was celebrated as an overnight village hero for organising such a lucrative and successful Sandauni event. There was no mistaking Uncle Charlie as he proudly paraded through the village streets with all the children running after him chanting, "Uncle Charlie! Uncle Charlie!" With a broad smile splashed all over his face, he began to walk with a swagger and a kind of exaggerated limp. Beaming Charlie had made a killing with one of the prettiest girls, and with his Sandauni mega-budget, he managed to arrange a quick wedding and pay dowry before departing back to the Nchanga copper mines with his new wife.

After that memorable Sandauni, there were numerous announcements of engagements and weddings, and then the Katobole saga continued as never before!

CHAPTER FOURTEEN

KALE KANYA MUKOWA, THE WITCHCRAFT CLEANSER

The adults in our village could sometimes be nervous and easily frightened, especially the elderly ones. I remember a day on which I had never seen so many elderly people, some using walking sticks, others dragging their feeble swollen feet, and stopping every now and again on their way towards Grandad's big house. Whoever managed to reach the steps leading to his veranda was quickly ushered in by a strange man with a long, black beard whom I had never seen before. He held in his hand a whip which looked like a dried cow or horse tail. As the elderly person reached the entrance, the strange man dipped the dry tail into a clay pot and flicked sacred water all over the stooped, nervous entrant who quickly disappeared into the round living room where Grandad was waiting for them.

Grandad's house was a big, round building made from burnt bricks. It had a round sitting room in the middle of the house, which was where adults used to sit and discuss their private adult issues or drink beer together. Then there was a passage around the entire house. Grandad's bedroom was at the far right of the house while the granddaughters used the middle portion of the passage and the grandsons used the other far end of the passage. A large kitchen was accessed from the round sitting room onto the massive veranda; on the left side of the veranda was the kitchen which was nearly as big as the sitting room. From the kitchen there were low steps leading to the road which led down the hill to the rest of the village. The house had been deliberately built on a levelled ant hill from where we could stand on the veranda and watch people coming to the house. Then we would run inside and report to Grandad or Grandma who was coming up the hill.

But this day was different. The elderly men and women who trudged up the road to Grandad's house appeared solemn and some had tears running down their harshly wrinkled faces. Crowds of people started to form in front of Grandad's house, mostly women with their babies on their backs. Grandma held my hand with such force that I begged her to let me go. I thought there was something sinister about these elderly peoples' mission to Grandad's house.

What I did not know was that at dawn, Grandad had made an announcement to the entire village that Kalekanya Mukowa, the 'witchcraft cleanser', was visiting Katobole village and everybody should hand over their witchcraft charms to Grandad before Kalekanya's arrival. Anyone found in possession of any witchcraft charms would receive his ruthless, deadly punishment. Kalekanya's known methods included administering poisonous cocktails to the offenders – which resulted in violent bouts of vomiting and often, death. His cruelest treatment was that he instructed those he found practising witchcraft to be buried alive. Such practices frightened people to their very bones and so they volunteered to bring their witchcraft charms to Grandad, who in turn would hand them over to Kalekanya. It was said that he would then destroy them, but who knows? Maybe cunning Kalekanya kept them for himself!

Out of the blue, I saw the solemn face of a man I knew passing by on his way into Grandad's house for said ritual. I relaxed my hand, then managed to pulled away from my grandmother's grip; she almost fell over as she rushed forward to grab me, this time grasping the back of my dress. She gave me that knowing look of "don't you dare!" and held both my hands tightly to prevent my escape. I begged Grandma, pleading through my sobs, that I wanted to greet Mr Ka-la-la and ask him what he was doing at Grandad's house.

"Do you know him?" Grandma coaxingly asked.

"Yes, yes, yes!" I answered. "He is my mother's uncle who once came home and ate *nshima* without washing his hands!" I told her.

It is a Zambian practice that people should wash their hands before they start eating *nshima*. On one occasion, the women or girls who served the meal to the man in question failed to adhere to a very well-known, unwritten law of providing water for washing hands before the main meal is brought to the table. A dish of water for washing hands is usually placed on the table before *nshima* and a relish of cooked meat is served.

So, people like my mother's uncle were most likely to attract some scorn, especially from children. Hence, as children we laughed at Mr Ka-la-la every time we saw him and teased him as 'the greedy man who eats *nshima* without washing his hands'. We nicknamed him Ka-la-la or something like that, although I can't remember exactly what that name meant.

I have to add here that I was impressed the last time I was in Zambia at how this old tradition has been adopted as a fashionable feature in most modern, newly-built homes. Many educated and wealthy Zambian individuals like to have a hand basin with running water appropriately installed in a corner of the dining room area so there is no longer any need to wait for the traditional dish of water to be brought to the table.

However, not to be beaten by those wealthy people, less well-off, self-taught welders or metal engineers have come up with something almost as good, and certainly more inventive. Many poorer households boast an iron stand with a tap in the corner of their dining room, and neatly installed below it, a bucket or basin serving the same purpose as the installations in the modern houses.

Thanks to these self-taught engineers, these stands can be bought from roadside sellers anywhere in Zambia, providing a perfect and more affordable household asset.

I must confess that I approve of this new invention which upholds and promotes a long-held traditional ritual in a modern and sophisticated way. It is a simple but essential way to prevent the spread of germs when touching food or visiting sick friends.

Anyway, I saw and remembered Mr Ka-la-la, and I wanted to throw myself on him so he could throw me in the air as he playfully did each time he saw me. Alas, this was not the time for silly games; it was a very serious looking Ka-la-la who had just passed by with his head bent down, ignoring any silly girls trying to throw themselves at him.

This procession of going into Grandad's house and being splashed with sacred water continued for some hours. After handing over their charms, some people came away in tears, others looked around nervously for their families, then hastily slipped away.

The Scary, Wobbly Man
with a Strange Charm

All of a sudden, a rough-looking old man with strange, sharp, evil eyes appeared. He was dressed in worn-out blue overalls, carrying a wooden box about the size of a briefcase. He seemed to be in a terrible hurry and all the women watched in amazement; no-one else was in such a hurry. He seemed to be struggling with his baggage and almost bumped into the strange man at the door with the long, black beard. The clay pot of sacred water was knocked over. The man was very unsteady on his feet and could barely manage to stand, let alone walk. His face was twisted in pain and agony and he seemed near to fainting at any time. There were gasps from the crowd of "Ooh! Look at that man! What's the matter with him? Eeeh! Eeeh! What is he carrying?"

Then an enraged Grandad emerged from the house onto the veranda dressed in his favourite white overalls, together with a checked jacket and complete with his treasured old Scottish colonial hat with black tassels. He looked around at the crowd, his face twisted in anger and urgency, and he harshly and hastily asked for some goat's milk and chicken eggs to be fetched quickly. Then he turned to the wobbly man and invited him to sit down.

"This man has brought his Ilomba charm (ritual charm snake)," announced Grandad.

The Ilomba is one of the most feared charms in Zambian tradition. It is said to be a sea snake with a human face and destructive powers. It takes on the identity of the person who owns it and needs to be fed on eggs, goat's milk and human blood from foetuses. If it dies, the owner feels the pain too and then dies.

"The snake is very tired and hungry," continued Grandad. "It is about to die and that's why this man here is also suffering. Please give the man some water to drink before he passes away."

Then the crowd became very agitated, shouting, "Ooh! No! No! Please, do not give food to that snake, eeeh! Please, let it die and let the owner die as well!"

Pointing at the bewildered, feeble man they said, "This man has killed so many people in this village using his snake! He makes pregnant women miscarry so that he can feed his snake on the foetuses! The man is a devil, let him die, eeeh! Eeeh!"

Others shouted, "Let him die! Why has he been hiding and left it too late to hand in his baby-eater devilish snake? He is an evil man! Let that man and his hideous snake die!"

Then one or two women came running up and handed something to Grandad who quickly went back inside the house.

A few minutes later, mysteriously, the fainting man got up, walked steadily out of Grandad's house and started walking away towards the village, without his box. The crowd continued booing and cursing him, sure that the snake must have been fed and hence the owner had also recovered.

I started worrying about the witchcraft charms being collected in Grandad's house. I asked Grandma where Grandad would put them. She told me he would take them to a sacred place where only Kalekanya would have access to them. For me that was not a good enough answer. I started wondering if Grandad was feeding that man's snake! I decided not to go near him or hug him anymore. In fact, I decided I would not enter Grandad's house ever again. I only changed my mind when Grandma assured me that not even Grandad could handle or touch the snake. Only the man with the whip, who would sprinkle sacred water on it to pacify it, could handle it or feed it.

Despite all the well-intentioned assurances from Grandma, I could not sleep a wink that night as I kept dreaming of bright lights and people dressed in funny outfits dancing around me. It was like a 'Thriller' night – now I think of Michael Jackson's stage troupe! I do not know how many times Grandma came over to have a look at the screaming, frightened Bupe.

I decided to exaggerate and amplify my sickness to another level by continually coughing and sneezing so that Grandma would sit and stay with me throughout the night. By early morning, I overheard Grandma making arrangements for me to be dispatched to my parents as I was not well; I had coughed and sneezed throughout the night, she moaned. That was exactly what I wanted to hear. And off I went home. When I told my mother about the village rituals and snakes and old people almost fainting, she was not amused and she was angry with Grandma for exposing me to such things. Grandma apologised and made light of the whole thing, so I stayed for one week with my parents while I was being attended to. But as you might expect, there were times when I used to forget all about my faked illness and would run around like a headless chicken until I was quickly called back in and given some more tablets.

When I eventually returned to Katobole village, there were endless stories of Kalekanya's visit to the village and how he had found some more witchcraft charms in certain houses – the owners had been dealt with accordingly. However, I did not ask any more questions because my parents were staunch Christians who were not happy that I had been allowed to witness such evil events. I was therefore forbidden from joining in any conversations concerning Kalekanya or witchcraft charms with my cousins on my return to Katobole village. Up to the present day, I do not know where Kalekanya came from, or what became of the charms he collected from the villagers.

While researching for this book, I wanted to interview some people on this subject but they were reluctant to speak. They were probably worried about the concerns of those families who were affected, as it brought a lot of shame on them and their offspring and they did not want to be scorned by others. Others discreetly advised me to let what happened in the past remain in the past.

Sometimes even writers can oblige that old French concept of 'laissez-faire', roughly translated as 'let sleeping dogs lie.'

CHAPTER FIFTEEN

TAX COLLECTOR'S NOTEBOOK

None of us can escape some form of taxation in this world. It was mentioned in the Bible as far back as the days of Abraham and Moses. "A tenth of the produce of the earth is to be consecrated and set apart for special purposes as a duty before God," it says in the book of Genesis.

Today we accept it as a fact of life.

My Africans ancestors didn't escape it; Grandad told me how the chief or king was held in high esteem and taxes of a sort were paid to royalty in the form of land, cattle and other objects of value, even human beings.

But when Africa was colonised by Europeans, the African way of life changed forever. The influence of those Western societies changed the lifestyle, the education of children, healthcare, and local government for my granddad's people.

The colonialists brought taxation to Zambia based on the British taxation system. Just like the medieval peasants, individuals had to pay rent for their land and a tithe to the church – ten per cent of the value of what their farm had produced in a year. The tithe could be paid either in cash or by giving up some of their produce, such as seeds, or equipment, but it was a hardship on the African families.

The Nine-To-Five Principle

The history books say that the African Villagers' Hut Tax was one of the central pillars of colonisation. The European powers wanted the colonies to pay their own way, and for Africans to enter into the cash economy by engaging in nine-to-five manual labour jobs. Taxation was a way of driving the men into menial jobs, working for white men for money which would enable them to pay the imposed Hut Tax. It had the added bonus of controlling unruly masses of people by keeping them busy in jobs all day, hence preventing them from roaming about in the streets causing mischief.

In Zambia, for example, in the 1940s and 1950s, colonial police would check on households at night, apprehending unemployed males. Every male was issued an ID (Icitupa) equivalent to today's NI number, and those found without such an ID were arrested and sent to colonial prisons. Hence it is not surprising that eventually there was unrest and bloody rebellion against the Hut Tax in most African colonies.

White Man's Dream is African Man's Blood

One such man had a vision of Britain controlling the African continent "from the Cape to Cairo". This was adventurer and diamond magnate Cecil John Rhodes, and in 1911 my grandfather's homeland was re-named Northern Rhodesia after him. Cecil Rhodes established the capital city at Livingstone, overlooking the Victoria Falls.

However, Cecil Rhodes' British South African Company did not have generous motives. Zambian rulers were presented with treaties of submission to give up their land, but these were often obtained by fraud and deceit and those rulers who resisted were dealt with by force.

During that time, there were a number of small gold and copper mines but they did not generate much profit. So Rhodes imposed the African Hut Tax on all African males from the age of puberty. This tax, about £2 per person, which then was a month's wages for an African labourer, had been a money-spinner in South Africa where Rhodes had worked before. Any resistance was suppressed with bullets; those who couldn't pay had their houses burnt down and those who ran away were imprisoned if caught.

In Zambia, for example, thousands of men were forced to leave their homes, and families had to go and work in Southern Rhodesian mines, just to be able to pay the Villagers' Hut Tax. The tax did some good though, as some money generated from it was used to finance construction of a railway line between Victoria Falls and Katanga in Zaire, which served as a lifeline for goods sent or received via ports on the south-western coast, on the Atlantic Ocean. But it made people angry at being forcibly removed from their homes to make way for the railways and farms for white settlers. As far as the Africans were concerned, colonial rule was a form of apartheid under which Africans were subjected to racial discrimination.

African Village Hut Tax Rebellions

In 1902, a tax collection exercise in Bailundo, now central Angola, went badly wrong when the local people rebelled violently, attacking African tax collectors and European traders.

In Sierra Leone, the imposition of tax on individual property was the final straw for local chiefs who had seen the British seizing any land that had no title deeds, appointing district commissioners to interfere with their local government and increasing levels of policing.

Northern Rhodesia and the African Villagers' Hut Tax

Many personal stories have been told of how the Hut Tax affected families in Northern Rhodesia. For example, there was a story told to me by a very respectable gentleman who witnessed, as a young man growing up in a Zambian village, cases of dishonesty, misconduct, abuse, and humiliation inflicted on African villagers by the tax collectors, or kapasos, and their white colonial masters.

He said in some cases, frightened, penniless husbands who could not afford to pay the tax were forced to trade in-kind their wives for sexual favours to kapasos who persisted in demanding payment of tax from defaulters. He told of a village scandal, where a husband took a night's refuge in a maize storage barn, or *ubutala,* while the kapaso raped his wife in their marital house throughout the night. The following morning, the kapaso returned to his administrative office and reported that the tax defaulter had died or moved on to another area.

The ill-treatment continued for years. African labourers went on strike against unfair taxes, with little result, but certainly loss of life. In 1948, the First African Mine Workers' Union was formed, and in 1955 there was a complete stoppage over pay conditions that lasted 58 days – ending with victory for the miners. Finally, the mining companies began moving Africans into management positions.

It wasn't until the late fifties, with the rise of younger and more active nationalists who were mostly educated in missionary schools, that the United National Independence Party emerged, led by Kenneth Kaunda, a charismatic activist and former school teacher. In October 1964, Zambia became an independent republic with Kenneth Kaunda as its first Republican president.

Southern Rhodesia and the African Villagers' Hut Tax

The Ministry of Foreign Affairs in Ghana published a report to the UN Security Council in early 1960, entitled 'Britain's Responsibility in Southern Rhodesia', admitting that the chief purpose of repression by taxation was "not only to secure revenue for the British South Africa Company, but also to force from the reservations, and to make available to Europeans, African labour".

Speaking to a couple of friends of Zimbabwean origin, they confirmed to me that their fathers and grandfathers in the late 1940s and 50s were subjected to a quarterly levy of £2 per head, for the African Hut Tax. One man vividly remembered that in 1956, when his father passed away, his mother was asked to pay £2 to have her deceased husband's name deregistered at the native colonial administrative office. My friend said his widowed mother had no money to pay the tax collector and when she was threatened with imprisonment as a tax defaulter, she went and begged for money from her church which was run by the London Mission Society.

This gentleman also confirmed that in rural districts of Southern Rhodesia there were cases where men who had no money and no means to raise the £2 quarterly levy, had to hide in thick forests for days before the arrival of the colonial tax collector, as failing to pay the levy carried a heavy prison sentence.

In another sad incident, my Zimbabwean friend remembered the story of an African farmer who killed and burned the body of a Mthunywa yi Nkosi who had pursued him for payment of the unpaid Hut Tax.

He said the African messenger had arrived at the defaulter's village looking for him. He was informed that the man he was looking for was cutting and burning stocks of his maize crop in a nearby field. The Mthunywa yi Nkosi proceeded to the cornfield and found the unsuspecting man. On seeing the tax collector and noticing that he was alone, the farmer came up with a deadly plan. He picked up his axe and approached the Mthunywa yi Nkosi. The defaulter pretended to be begging and pouring praises on his unsuspecting victim. When the defaulter got within inches of the flattered and smiling tax collector, he sprang at him, swinging his axe and chopping his body into pieces.

He then picked up the severed body parts and burnt them, together with the dried maize stocks. And so the tax collector disappeared without a trace.

It was only when the case of the missing Mthunywa yi Nkosi was re-opened a few years later that other officers retraced the last movements of the colleague in question. They therefore interviewed the last man he had spoken to. The farmer denied any knowledge of meeting the tax collector as he had been in his fields burning maize stock on that day. The officers then asked the defaulter to take them to the field where he had been working. Within a few hours, the sharp-eyed policemen discovered a police officer's old burnt out belt buckle, charred silver shirt buttons and some burnt out human bones, all at the same spot in the field. The defaulter was arrested and re-interviewed. He confessed to the killing for which he was given a death sentence and was later hanged by the white colonialists.

The Beaten-up Old Grey-Green Land Rover

I have a recollection of my own about the African Villagers' Hut Tax.

One day, a grey-green beaten up old Land Rover came roaring into the village. Before it had even stopped, a short, stout white man jumped out, his two bodyguards right behind him, and started walking at a very high speed towards Grandad's veranda where chairs and stools had been arranged in a neat line. Grandma held me tight as I tried to get closer so I could look at the white man's twisted black moustache which resembled a cow's horns or a bicycle's handlebars. I also wondered why the white man was walking so fast and not paying attention or acknowledging people who were by now dancing to welcome him. He strode straight across the well-manicured lawn and jumped the two steps leading up to the veranda. Without waiting to be invited he chose to sit on the highest chair and Uncle Samuel sat next to him. The two greeted each other in a strange language which I could not understand. All I heard was, "Yes sir, yes sir." *What is the white man saying to Uncle Samuel to which he is answering only yes sir, yes sir?* I was thinking. Then Grandad appeared, gingerly negotiating the two steps while leaning heavily on his walking stick, and sat on a stool next to his son who introduced him to the white man. So Uncle Samuel was the translator to Grandad – clever Uncle, he could speak the white man's language. Grandad was dressed in a red overall, with an oversized Scottish plaid jacket on top. He was wearing his favourite red colonial Scottish hat with black tassels flowing from the top. Grandad took the hat off when greeting the white man then put it back on again. Grandad looked very impressive, and next to him the fierce-looking tax collector looked like a frustrated pirate.

The Tax Collector's Notebook

Once settled, the tax collector wasted no time and pulled out his notebook, saying something to Uncle Samuel who translated it to Grandad. I saw Grandad frown a bit and then say something to his son, who in turn said, "Sorry Bwana, the man in question died," or, "Sorry Bwana, that man went mad or suffered from leprosy and is locked up in his hut for fear of spreading it to other villagers."

Then all of a sudden, the women dancers started to pick up their children and run away. Grandma tightened her grip on me also, but before I had time to ask what was happening, I saw Chapa (an aggressive schizophrenic in the village) charging towards the veranda where the white man and Grandad were sitting. The white man's kapasos and able-bodied young men from the village tackled Chapa and threw him down to the ground. They quickly tied him up and marched him away from the gathering. Some of the women and children were weeping quietly. Grandma squeezed my hand to reassure me that everything was fine.

The white man flinched, then continued calling out names of men from a long list in his notebook. Grandad continued to update him sadly with details of dead men, or others who had succumbed to various deadly illnesses. In the end, Grandad handed over money he had collected from his eligible subjects. I watched the white man thrust wads of notes into a long grey sack (to me it looked like a Santa sack). I was wondering whether anybody had counted that money. How did Grandad know how much he had given the white man? And where was the money going anyway? Why had the white man or his kapasos not counted the money?

I pondered silently and in my childish head I hoped that the tax collector counted the money and then gave some back to Grandad for the big job he had done in collecting it well in advance from his impoverished subjects. Later, I asked Grandad where the white man took the money to, and he answered me straight to the point: "The money is remitted to the white man's mother country." I kept quiet as I did not know what that meant at the age I was then.

The white man came to the end of his session, and murmured something to Uncle Samuel who translated it to Grandad. I saw Grandad saying something with tears welling in his eyes. I wondered what kind of exchange was going on. I was later told that the white man was passing his condolences to Grandad on losing so many young men to incurable diseases and untimely premature deaths.

Grandad then instructed Uncle Samuel to present gifts to the white man, some of which had been displayed nicely on long woven trays. There were artefacts, woven crafts, mats, nicely decorated walking sticks, live chickens, and some sort of black-grey stones – maybe manganese?

Then the white man was invited to join in the dancing as the women had returned and the drumming and whirling reached its climax. For the first time, the white man smiled, then stretched himself and jokingly joined the circle of teenage girls, who by now could be seen provocatively shaking and wiggling their waists like leeches thrust into a bowl of fresh water.

A few minutes later, the white man and his entourage disappeared in their old grey-green Land Rover.

The Celebrations

Everybody breathed a sigh of relief and the drumming and dancing continued into the small hours of the night. The men, who had dressed roughly to appear as imbeciles to avoid the African Villagers' Hut Tax, washed and dressed up decently and came to join the party. The merry atmosphere was only broken by random fights started by jealous spouses, or by the persistent arguments my grandad's nephew Chamutobo picked with other men whom he perceived to be ignorant and uneducated.

The following morning, those who had disguised themselves as imbeciles started arriving at Grandad's house to thank him for saving them from paying the African Hut Tax, and more importantly, for saving them from being sent to colonial prisons for their failure to pay.

A Custodial Sentence

I have another tale to tell about the African Villagers' Hut Tax; this was told to me by my sister-in-law, Chalwe Bwalya, who now lives and works in Manchester. After reading the draft notes I was making for this book and becoming interested, she recounted what her late mother had told her of how the African Villagers' Hut Tax had affected the Bwalya family.

The area where Chalwe grew up lies at the foot of Muchinga Escarpment, a very hilly region. It is near Ching'ombe Mission in Luena Valley, Central Province of Zambia. Even today, roads in the area become impassable in the rainy season so one can imagine the state of those roads during the colonial era, 50 to 60 years ago.

In around 1960, Chalwe's mother witnessed a very odd occurrence. The vehicle – it might have been a grey-green beaten up old Land Rover carrying a white colonial tax collector – had broken down. Probably at the expectation of indulgent white colonialists, the villagers were being asked to carry the white man on their shoulders using a hammock called *amacila*. Since Chalwe's father was a well-known hunter in the area, he was chosen to be one of the hammock carriers.

However, Chalwe's father was a very proud and stubborn man who considered his wife's Lala people to be too passive and fearful of the white colonialists. He had migrated from Luapula Valley in North East Zambia but was married to a Lala woman and had thereafter moved into Central Province, the Lala-occupied region. Mr Bwalya might have been radicalised whilst growing up in Luapula Valley where politics regarding Zambia's independence were rife and volatile. Hence Mr Bwalya had been instilled with a fighting spirit, to stand up for the country's freedom and independence. Whilst in his wife's

Lala-occupied territory, he had probably ruffled some feathers with his highly political views. This led to him being a regular suspect whenever any political disturbances took place in the area.

Chalwe said that, as a result of her father's open condemnation of white colonialism, he was constantly monitored by the sharp-eyed white men's informers and became a target. His categorical refusal to ferry the white man in a hammock was perceived as being politically motivated, therefore action had to be taken before he was able to spread his bitter hatred for white colonialists to other villagers in the area.

Chalwe's father was to be harshly punished in order to create a deterrent to others who may have tried to join him in his calls for a free and independent country and to wipe out all white colonialists. The unrepentant Mr Bwalya was therefore summoned to attend court. His offence of refusing to ferry a white man was taken very seriously and a custodial sentence was imposed on him. It was agreed that the penalty for this most deviant and disloyal offence was six months' imprisonment 'with hard labour' and thereafter Mr Bwalya, the prisoner, was taken and locked away in a prison somewhere in a distant province.

Positive Outcome from a Colonial Custodial Prison Sentence

Chalwe told me that her mother gave the positive side of her husband's custodial sentence and the time he spent in prison. According to her late mother, at the time of Mr Bwalya's release, her husband looked very well and had put on a lot of weight. 'Where there is a will, there is a way,' they say, so despite his humiliation and the most unjust punishment, Mr Bwalya's spirit was not crushed. He utilised his empty time to carry out menial jobs which gave him enough income to buy clothes for his wife and children on his release. In short, this proud, brave and charismatic Luapula man maintained his pride and his status of being head and provider to his beloved family, even in the confines of a dark colonial prison cell. Most of all, Chalwe's mother was impressed by her husband's ability to continue caring for and thinking of providing for his family during his imprisonment.

Chalwe and I laughed our heads off. Firstly, we were surprised that a family man could be sent to prison for refusing to ferry a colonial tax collector in a hammock. The question we kept asking ourselves was, "Couldn't an able-bodied white colonial man walk independently? Why did he request to be carried on other people's shoulders in a hammock?" We both concluded that the colonialists at that time possessed an arrogance and punishing attitude which fortunately we don't see in their offspring, as today's white man seems eager to prove to the world that they possess a natural knowledge and strength to do and conquer anything, be it climbing the Himalayas or wading singlehandedly through wild African rivers. Today's white man, suffering a mishap involving the breakdown of a vehicle in wildest Africa, would lead the way out of his predicament, walking boldly on foot, partly to benefit from the exercise, but also to show the world that he is a 'manly man', a different species, a conqueror who is there to set an example to the primitive people of foreign lands.

Chalwe and I both agreed that in a layman's eyes, the punishment for the offence Mr Bwalya had committed far outweighed the severity of the crime.

We wondered, too, how one can put on weight whilst incarcerated, since the usual perception of prison life is hard work, little or no sleep, food deprivation, abuse, illness and punishment, to mention just a few of the hardships. Then we thought about the lifestyle of an ancient African villager who would leave home at dawn, go out hunting or fishing or farming on an empty stomach with no time for breakfast, and only eat one meal at night time. A prison sentence would make a difference to his diet and eating routine. We realised that Mr Bwalya would have been served three meals a day, and just having a few minutes of not worrying or rushing to provide for his family might have given him some relaxation time, so in a strange way he benefited from his imprisonment. This is just one example of how some Zambian people and their families became embroiled in the evils of the colonialist era.

Mother of All Sins

Writing about the African Villagers' Hut Tax now, and considering the various ways in which hard-pressed villagers managed to evade paying it to the merciless white tax collectors, gives me mixed feelings. On one hand, I am pleased at the ingenuity of African village headmen or leaders of that difficult era and generation, to save their poor subjects from lengthy prison sentences for failure to pay the heavy levies demanded by their colonial masters.

On the other hand, I am trying to think of the positives which came out of this. The first thing which springs to mind is financial discipline. Would African countries have benefited more if they had continued to pay the Village Hut Tax after gaining independence from the British government, and used that money for improvements of schools, roads, and health centres? Village cleanliness: did this practice of cleaning, repairing and repainting houses, digging lavatories before the arrival of white tax collectors, enhance the villagers' standard of living? If such routines were continued after independence, would it have improved and promoted health and social care at African village level? Accountability: who was accountable for the money collected from African villagers? Who benefited most from the African Hut Tax? What lessons were learnt from the introduction of the tax from both the African and the colonialist perspectives?

At this point I leave the entire debate to the readers of this book to judge who had the last laugh – Grandad and his cunning, brainy, village imbecile impersonators, or the feisty, wealth-driven colonialists?

CHAPTER SIXTEEN

CHIPILI GIRLS' BOARDING SCHOOL

Like any other pupil, I found it nerve-wracking and at the same time exciting to be informed by our primary school teachers that our school had been chosen, with others, to send bright pupils to study at one of the better boarding schools run by the Anglican Church.

However, as a condition, it was compulsory for the under-elevens from chosen schools to sit a Selection Examination from which a few successful boys and girls would be chosen to attend the then prestigious missionary boarding schools.

Entry examinations took place in May, and by July the results were out, in time for the new term in September. During colonial days, Zambian school calendars ran concurrently with the British ones. As a result, all school terms started in September of each year, and O-Level Examinations were marked at Cambridge and certificates were printed with the Cambridge University logo. However, all this changed after independence in 1964.

The day when the results were announced was a big day in the school calendar, attended by parents who were anxious to receive their children's results. As for my uncle Mr Mukundubili, it was a day of pride; dressed in a smart suit, he walked around with his head high, strutting along like the head lion of a jungle pride. Many of the parents tried to pass close by him, superstitiously believing that brushing against him or being noticed by him would help their children pass and be selected to go to a boarding school. Little did they know that the papers had already been marked and the headmaster already had in his hands the results of those who had passed the examinations. In any case, it was said that teachers swapped papers or cunningly gave good results to their own children or a few favoured pupils.

Some pupils and their parents were already in floods of tears. Being related to a headmaster was a great advantage, for my mother had already been secretly advised that I had passed. But quite rightly, nothing was mentioned to me, hence the apprehension and anxiety of the day were unbearable.

Eventually the headmaster of the primary school announced the under-elevens' examination results. The headmaster also announced the names of the pupils who were selected to go and study at the prestigious boarding schools. Somehow, amidst the commotion and excitement, my name was called first to receive a medal for scoring the highest mark in the examinations, and secondly, to congratulate me and my parents for having achieved a place at Chipili Girls' Boarding School! I think that was the best day in my young life; it felt like winning the jackpot!

I cannot remember if I danced or cried but I remember running home with the envelope containing the results in my hands. I could not trust anybody with my results and I would not even give the envelope to my mother who had attended the ceremony. I wanted to take it to my father myself. I just wanted to tell him that I had passed and then hand over the envelope to him.

My father had become ill immediately after I sat for my under-elevens examination and was unable to attend the ceremony where our results were announced. Moreover, he had to leave our village for treatment in neighbouring Zaire, a few weeks before I left for Chipili Girls' Boarding School.

My Late Brother John

When I think back to that day, it would have been more natural and comforting for me had my father escorted me to the new school. Unfortunately, he was too ill; he just managed to gather my boarding school fees of £9.00 and immediately left for his treatment in Zaire, currently known as the Democratic

Republic of Congo. The responsibility of taking me to a new school fell on my elder brother John who, himself, was barely in his late teens. He was the eldest and therefore had to take over the running of things in Dad's absence, which included ensuring that I attend my new school on time. My father was a self-taught entrepreneur, who, after retiring from his police job, ran various small businesses, such as a village store and marketing co-operatives, and was also involved with manganese mining companies in the area.

Boarding School Bullying

Like any other child, I did not want to leave my home and my friends for a new school in a faraway district. I was apprehensive and afraid of the unknown. I was frightened at the thought of meeting new teachers and pupils, and I had also been told about missionaries and their rigid regimes. However, this journey into the unknown was my first step into a world of unlimited travel and adventures.

Prior to my enrolment at Chipili Girls' Boarding School, I was told about the strict religious regimes which were imposed on boarders by white missionaries. For example, I was warned about morning prayers which started at dawn. I was also warned about certain religious calendar dates such as Good Friday, Easter Monday and many others on which pupils were expected to pray throughout the day, without being served any hot meals.

Most of all, I was anxious about the challenges of attending a school which was run by the Anglican Church while my parents practised a different religion. I worried about the possibility of not being able to sing their songs and not being able to say the Lord's Prayer. I also worried about other children taking the Mickey out of me. In the sixties, particularly in Zambian boarding schools, bullying of new pupils was widespread. The fact that I was the only girl chosen from my school to attend Chipili Girls' Boarding School that year did not help matters. It left me feeling lonely and vulnerable. However, I later learnt that there were boys from my area at the boys' boarding school, including my cousin, the late Frank Miyambo, whose father was my father's half-brother, who had settled with the other branch of the family along Luongo River, near Musonda Falls.

The School Premises

As far as the missionaries were concerned, the boys' school was a different entity from the girls' boarding school. We lived on different premises and only met during Mass at church, or in shops or in the hospital, or during interschool game competitions. For the girls, the boys' compound was out of bounds and vice-versa; anybody caught trespassing was heavily punished. Being found in the boys' or girls' dormitory led to instant dismissal from the school. A few boys and girls were expelled for being caught in the wrong place at the wrong time.

On reflection, the missionaries had double standards or rather contradicted themselves. For example, running concurrently to the girls' and boys' boarding schools was a school for the blind which was just as big as the two other boarding schools. However, the blind school was a co-educational establishment; boys and girls lived in the same premises. They ate in the same dining halls and attended the same classes. We often saw them walking in mixed groups of boys and girls to church, or going for baths at the Lufubu River. What made the missionaries think that blind pupils could mix and interact freely while sighted ones were kept apart? There were stories that quite a sizeable number of blind girls fell pregnant and were expelled from school just as many sighted ones were. However, in the eyes of the missionaries, only sighted pupils needed to be watched for any form of naughtiness with the opposite sex.

Beautiful Bungalows
on a Rocky Plateau

After travelling by bicycle for over seven hours, crossing more than four rivers and traversing dense forests inhabited by lions and leopards, my brother and I finally arrived at Chipili Mission. My brother asked for directions to the girls' boarding school and we headed uphill to where it was situated. The scenery was breathtaking. With hindsight I quite understand why white missionaries had chosen this mountainous plateau to be the headquarters of the Anglican Church in the Province.

Lufubu River and its Thunderous Waterfalls

The Mission station was built on a plateau fronted by beautiful hills, and on rocky slopes in between the hills runs the Lufubu River whose rapids form a waterfall which flows westward into the misty valleys below. The waterfall makes a thunderous noise which can be heard miles away.

Across the river is a long bridge, constructed where the valleys form a narrow passage. The bridge is enormous with high steel rails on both sides and wide footpaths for pedestrians and cyclists. This bridge forms a boundary between the south side of the river where the mission station is situated, consisting of the girls' and boys' boarding schools, the Blind School, the hospital and the church, and the north side where there are shops, residential houses, bus terminals, a market and other villages dotted about along the hillside as far as the eye can see.

Standing on the plateau which houses the Mission station, one can see gallons and gallons of water falling into the rocky valleys, forming a misty cloud down below. Unknown to me on that day was the fact that I would soon be diving into this waterfall. Jumping from the bridge ten or twenty feet above the water, and then swimming in the swift currents towards the waterfall was unimaginable to me until I actually started doing it with the other girls. All the girls and boys dived and swam in the mighty waters, especially in the rainy months when the river overflows. We would queue up along the bridge to jump into the fast flowing river below. And then we would cling to the rocks on the river banks before the mighty waterfall thundered into the deep ravine below. It was scary to start with, but soon I became an expert at it and enjoyed it very much. It was our pastime and we loved it. Fortunately, during the four years I spent at Chipili Girls' Boarding School, I never heard of any accident involving a pupil being swept away or anything like that.

Writing about it now, I can feel the hairs standing up on the back of my neck and my heart beating faster and faster. I am horrified that we were allowed to dive into such dangerous waters at such an early age without any form of supervision. I would not allow my child to engage in such dangerous activity at all. Those were innocent years when tragedy and mishaps were not anticipated and we were blessed that nothing of that sort happened to anybody.

The Scented Pathways

Arriving at Chipili Girls' Boarding School in the company of my brother John, I respectfully followed while he led the way uphill to the imposing buildings in front of us. As I trod along the gravel road leading to the station high up on the plateau, I saw long buildings on the edge of the hill and a couple of big, beautifully built houses. Some had corrugated iron roofs and others were beautifully and professionally thatched bungalows. What caught my eye were those immaculate flower beds, the blossoming flowering plants and bushes all set along the small intersecting roads leading to each house. The scents and wild perfumes which filled my nostrils were hypnotising. I thought I must have reached paradise or heaven.

As I turned my gaze westward, I saw this most imposing building with protruding steel spires pointing upwards into the sky that seemed not to end until they met the clouds. I pointed to the building and asked my brother what it was. He simply turned round and said, "That is a church." It was the strangest church I had ever seen in my life. I thought of our church back home in the village which was merely a long, small building without any steel spires or crosses protruding high up into the sky.

My brother once more asked for directions for the girls' school's administration block. A few minutes later, we were standing on the steps of this long building on the edge of a rocky slope from where I could see tons of water rushing over the rocks and flowing into the steep slopes below. I was taken aback by the deafening sounds of the waterfall. My first thought was to cling to my brother so that he would not leave me behind. The whole place seemed strange and unfamiliar. While I was trying to make sense of my new environment, I did not realise that my brother was talking to a middle-aged white woman who had come out to meet us at the door.

I just heard my name being mentioned and the woman stepped forward to greet and welcome us into the building. Despite the circumstances of this new environment, I'm sure I managed to stretch my hand out to this woman who I later learnt was called Miss Lambert, the head of the girls' boarding school. After introducing me to the headmistress, my brother handed over the school fees which were £9.00, equivalent to about £900.00 today. Oh yes, the Zambian currency then was pounds sterling and shillings and pence. After handing over my small suitcase to this woman, my brother was thanked and asked to leave.

I tried very hard to hide my tears, but when I saw the back of my brother John I just burst into uncontrollable sobs. I cried for my father and mother whom I had not seen in a long while (as Dad had been taken to another country for hospital treatment). I cried for my brother who was my only source of comfort, and at that particular moment I thought that he would never come back for me again. I cried for myself as I was bewildered and did not know what to do in this place where I did not know anybody.

I must have cried myself to sleep because when I woke up late in the evening, I was on a single bed surrounded by four or five girls I did not know. One called my name and said, "This will be your dormitory and I am your prefect; I will look after you." But I started crying again. Then I heard a stern voice say, "Don't go near her, she is just a little girl, leave her alone." I felt fearful, wondering what the girls surrounding my bed might do to me. I coiled myself deeper into the small blanket covering me and awaited my fate.

All of a sudden, somebody pulled the blanket off me, and I thought, "Yes, this is it, I am dead, and the girls have attacked me!" For a moment I panicked but then I gathered some strength, and with my heart throbbing in my mouth, I opened my eyes and saw the white woman I had met when I arrived. Oh, thank God, it was Miss Lambert. She asked me to follow her. I got up from the bed and followed her to her office. She then called the girl who had introduced herself as my prefect. Her name was Hilda. Miss Lambert told Hilda to take me to the dining hall at tea-time. She also instructed me to stay with Hilda at all times. I said, "Yes madam," and left with Hilda holding my hand.

Hilda, who was much older than me, was a very nice girl. She secured my little case and asked me to sit with her all the time. I think she was protecting me from being bullied as a newcomer. She assisted me with a bath and later sat with me at the same table for the evening meal. From that day, Hilda became my principal carer and saviour. She even pretended we were related and told everybody that I was her lost cousin. My stay could not have been any better, and now that I was related to the prefect, I even became popular with other girls who wanted little favours from the prefect Hilda. That's life; one has to survive and sometimes one meets Good Samaritans in the most unexpected settings.

During a familiarisation walk, which took us around the Mission station, Hilda told me that the long buildings were dormitories, and the beautiful bungalows were teachers' and priests' houses. The most imposing building was an Anglican Church which was soon to become my second home and my favourite place. I felt at peace there, and would forget about the bullying and homesickness and I prayed to Almighty God with my childish purity and honesty.

Apart from the classroom, we pupils spent many hours in church during morning prayers, evening prayers, Sunday Mass, christenings, baptisms, funerals, wedding services and so on. Church-going was part of my existence during those years. As time passed, lone prayers became my escape and survival route and came to play a central part in my everyday life at Chipili Girls' Boarding School. Those same spiritual values I inherited at an early age have become an important cornerstone of my adult life.

Grace the Rebel

In spite of this, you will find out in later chapters that at a certain stage in my life I rebelled. This was just a cry for help or a way of finding the real me. I started questioning certain beliefs and values. For example, I was born to Jehovah's Witness parents and, as such, I learnt how to read the Bible before I could read a novel. Then I went to a Mission boarding school at the age of eleven where I was expected to kneel down and pray before 6 a.m. or before I had even opened my eyes. So when I finally went to a boarding secondary school where there were no forceful parents to ensure that I read the Bible before going to bed, nor white missionaries to ensure I attended Mass every morning, I stopped going to church altogether and threw away all the Bibles. In fact, I only started going back to church when I had my own children and became concerned that they might miss out on developing a spiritual ethos, and that they may grow up not having God in their lives.

My First Culture Shock

At Chipili Girls' Boarding School, I came across my first culture shock, as most of my new teachers were white missionaries who had a completely different middle-class value system from mine. To mention a few, we had Father Kingsnorth who was Head Priest and was responsible for all church activities. There was Miss Lambert who was head of the girls' school and taught different subjects. We also had monks and young priests whose names I cannot remember. In addition, there were African priests like Father Njamu Name, as well as African teachers like the meticulous Mr Titus Lumbwe who headed the boys' boarding school. Mr Lumbwe later rose in the ranks and held very senior posts in the Zambian Ministry of Education. There was also Mr Katontoka, whom I met again later in adult life and we became like niece and uncle.

One of the teachers who taught at the blind boarding school was Mr Mukaya Mukanga, and years later in London, our two families became very close. I met Mr Mukaya Mukanga on his appointment as First Secretary at the Zambia High Commission in London.

I dearly appreciated the kind of friendship which embraced our two families when we were in the UK, so far away from our native land and so far away from Chipili Mission where fate had brought us together. I felt as if I had a blood relative in London.

Unfortunately, Mr Mukanga passed away upon his return to Zambia in 2001. I still miss him and his family so much. The kind of friendship the two families enjoyed is simply not replaceable. MHSRIP.

There were of course prominent female African teachers at Chipili, like the late Auntie Mrs Mabula, married to the late Bishop Mabula. I have referred to Mrs Mabula as Auntie because during my Chipili days I grew up with some of the Mabula daughters, and together we went to Kasama Girls' Secondary School where we completed our secondary education. Hence one or two of the Mabula girls have remained good long-standing friends of mine. Although I rarely see them, they also live and work abroad; when we meet we are just like long-lost sisters and we have lots to catch up, on bless them.

There were other female teachers, for example my godmother, Agnes, who came from the Tonga tribe, which in the sixties was perceived as foreign. Tongas come from the Southern Province of Zambia and up to the present day it is quite a foreign land, many hundreds of miles away from Chipili Mission in Luapula Province. Tongas have their own dialect which is different from the Bemba language spoken in Northern Luapula, Copperbelt, Muchinga, and Central and mostly in Lusaka Provinces of Zambia. And the two tribes have very different cultures. However, things have eased a bit these days with the rise in inter-marriage amongst young people. My

Tonga godmother chose my baptism name for me, Prudence. Auntie Agnes became my spiritual inspiration and at the same time she was like a mother to me – she looked after me like her own child. I ate and slept at her house on weekends. She cared for me when I was unwell – what would I have done without her? She was my spiritual angel who fulfilled my spiritual, social and emotional needs at that time. Unfortunately, I lost contact with Auntie Agnes over the years. I just wish her well, wherever she is. God willing, one day I will go looking for her.

My Conversion to a New Faith

I was desperate to be accepted by the missionaries. The truth is, I was chosen to attend this Mission school because of my high marks and, once at the school, there were other requirements or expectations which I could not fulfill and life became extremely difficult for me. I decided I had to do something in order to continue with my education. So I made the decision to convert to the Anglican Church behind my parents' back.

It was not an easy decision, especially for an eleven-year-old girl, but sometimes one has to grow up overnight and make some very important decisions. I must confess, I kept my baptism and my new name secret from my parents. They have since died and I now feel guilty for not owning up, but I did not want to be the odd one out in the school and be singled out by both fellow pupils and missionaries.

I prayed about it and really I think I made the right decision because things became much easier for me afterwards. But I didn't ever tell my parents about my conversion; at the time, all of my brothers and sisters were petrified of our father including myself, and I didn't dare to imagine what would have happened if I had gone to him and said, "Dad, I am dishonouring your religion and beliefs." This was the man who paid my school fees and had very high hopes for me academically and I did not want to rub him up the wrong way.

Irrespective of their religion, I have always appreciated, respected and cherished my parents. I feel proud of having been born into a religion which imparted a lot of priceless moral and personal values to me. At the same time, I am proud of belonging to the Anglican Church from which I draw all my spiritual strength.

However, I do regret that I never disclosed my conversion to my parents. Had there been a good time and space to do so, and in hindsight, knowing now that my parents were both quite liberal, I feel they would have accepted the reasons why I had to do what I did.

The Faraway Promised Land

Being an Anglican School, Chipili Mission was directly connected to Canterbury in England, and for the first time in my life I became aware of places called England and Canterbury where all the good things came from. Every Sunday, there were announcements of motor vehicles, money, clothing or food being sent to our church school from England, or people visiting from Canterbury. From that time on, England and Canterbury became familiar words and, as a child, I became intrigued by those fascinating places which sounded so far away from my home, and yet brought a unique sense of closeness and a feeling of belonging. I felt as though I had already been to Canterbury or England. Unknown to me at the time was the fact that eventually I would travel to these places and that England would become my permanent adoptive country.

As mentioned earlier, there were always a lot of visitors to Chipili Mission from other areas. Most of them were from St Ignatius College in Mapanza in the Southern Province. St. Ignatius was also run by the Anglican Church. Although I have never been to Mapanza, the college there must be well thought of because I still hear people talk about it here in England and I was asked about it when I visited Virginia in the USA in 2008. We also had regular visitors from Canterbury, England. Some stayed for days, weeks or months and others remained much longer. We also had all sorts of Sunday visitors including white families from the provincial headquarters in Mansa, situated about 36 miles away, and others like white farmers, road building contractors, doctors and nurses, teachers and many other foreign families in the area, all coming to worship at the Anglican Church at Chipili Mission.

Beautiful Sundays

Sundays at Chipili Mission always saw big gatherings and the church was always full. There was a buzz of excitement and happiness amongst the pupils, the worshippers and even the priests. These gatherings looked to me like a miniature version of the gatherings at Ascot Races in England. White women and girls wore their very best clothes, their men and boys wore smart suits. The African women put on a display of colourful traditional attire and we pupils from the three boarding schools proudly wore our beautiful uniforms. Even the church service was colourful and beautiful with the priests dressed in their multi-coloured robes. The choirboys and the altar boys who carried burning candles were appropriately dressed, and most of all I felt exhilarated by the aroma of burning incense in the church. Sunday mornings were simply a spectacle worth watching and remembering today.

As a middle-class tradition, boarders were treated to a very special meal on Sundays. I wouldn't say that it was equivalent to a roast dinner, but I must confess it was something everybody looked forward to having on this special day.

Reminiscing on the Hard Times

In my first and second years at Chipili Boarding School, I had to put up with some financial hardships. As result of my father receiving treatment in Zaire (RDC) at that time, there was nobody to provide me with pocket money or any other financial support. My brother, who was looking after things in my father's absence, was probably under strict instructions not to misuse the little money upon which the family depended. As long as he came to pick me up at the end of term and took me back to school at the beginning of the new term that was fine with me. This meant I had only basic clothing and it was a luxury to have more than two sets of underwear! God forgive my childish mind; I thought that other children were treated like little princesses when their parents brought extra food parcels for them every weekend, or sent money to them in the post.

Having said that, such hardships didn't really matter to me as I just saw it as a normal way of life. It is only now as I am writing about it that I am feeling sorry for the little girl I was then. To be fair to her, Grace was just a bright, happy little poor kid who had no concerns in the world as long as she had her books to read. Her favourite subjects were Geography, History and English. She found it interesting to read about foreign lands and their peoples.

All my reading has come in handy to me as an adult, and I feel a sense of familiarity wherever I go in the world, for example when I visited the Shetland Islands I felt very excited about it all. But it was much more cosmopolitan than I had expected from my geography lessons of many years ago.

Wading Through Raging Floods for Education

One January day, my brother John and I set off very early in the morning. My brother was taking me back to school after the Christmas holidays. We noticed on the way that all the small rivers had flooded. Somehow, we took no notice and just continued on our journey. Eventually we met a man coming in the opposite direction. He stopped us and warned us about the reported floods at Chisamba River. I saw my brother's face drop but he assured the older man that we would be careful and that he would ensure we crossed Chisamba River safely. The older man tried to persuade us to go back but my brother would not listen. He thanked the older man and we left on our bicycle.

My brother John was a man of very few words. At the same time, he was calm and very reassuring. During those journeys, he would answer my millions of questions. He never lost his temper with me, nor did he ask me to shut up. I asked about whatever I saw, flowers, plants, forests, rivers, animals, villages on the way, and most of all I asked him about our father's health. I was very anxious and wanted my father back home. My brother had the ability to pick his words very carefully and, in his reassuring manner, he would say something like, "Yes Bupe, our father is all right. I just received a letter from him in which he said he will soon be coming home." Oh, God, I missed my father and my mother who had gone with him to the hospital in Zaire. I would choke on tears all the way back to school, but show no signs of distress to my brother.

On such trips, sometimes I occupied myself admiring budding flowers and plants on the way. I loved the Zambian January weather – it was the rainy season and everything was fighting to shoot out of the soil: mushrooms, flowers and grasses, and the birds were singing nonstop; there were also swarms of beautifully coloured butterflies. All the way the scenery was breathtaking.

However, after many hours of cycling, we reached the Chisamba River. And as the older man had warned us, it had broken its banks. I felt my heart jump into my mouth. I could not imagine how we were going to cross that river which looked like a big lake to me. I turned and looked at my brother who had knelt down to fold up his trouser legs. I asked him what we should do; perhaps we should return home? He said no, we would try to cross. I looked at him and started crying. I was afraid of water and I thought we were going to drown or get eaten up by crocodiles. I pleaded with him that there could be snakes and crocodiles in the river. My brother comforted me and said he would wade through the water first and then I would hang by the bicycle handlebars which he would carry on his shoulders. Just the thought of trying to cross in such fast flowing waters frightened the hell out of me. I told him I would not go with him; I would walk back home. "Would you know how to find your way home?" he asked me. I said yes, I would walk along the road. "And what will you do if you meet a lion or a leopard?" he asked me. Oh God, I looked behind me and ran towards him. I felt as if the lion or leopard was right there waiting to attack me. I said, "Oh please, please, do not leave me, I will come with you and cross the river with you!"

Naturally, at eleven years of age I was short and would have been easily swept away by the forceful river currents. However, my brother's devised plan of hanging on to the bicycle handlebars worked wonders. By the time I felt relaxed and was getting used to swimming alongside him, we were wading up the other side of the river bank. We were wading in waters which had risen to the level of my brother's shoulders. When we reached the opposite bank, my brother sat me down and heaved a big sigh of relief. He carefully held me and changed me into dry clothes which he had preserved securely in my small suitcase, and once again it was back on the bicycle to continue our journey to the Mission station. Ordinary people from villages on our route stopped us and asked how we had managed to cross the Chisamba River which had been reported to be flooded. When my brother told our story, the villagers were gobsmacked and warned him not to use the same route on his way back home. I am sure he must have taken their advice. I never did remember to ask my brother John how he got back home after escorting me to school during that rainy January month.

As a result of his added responsibilities in my father's absence, and because he had to work to sustain the family, my brother John lost many years of his own education. However, he later went back to school, passed his O-levels and continued studying by correspondence courses until he enrolled full time at the University of Zambia, where he was awarded a Diploma in Social Work.

Apart from taking me to and from the Mission school during school holidays, my brother once more came to my rescue in later life. Once again he stood in for our father who had finally died, and from then on John had the responsibility of paying for my secondary education and that of the younger siblings of the family. Brother John has always remained the head of our family. Each time I reflect on my past, as well as my life in general, I fail to find befitting words to express my heartfelt gratitude and appreciation for my brother, who, with his youthful determination and maturity in taking over our father's reins at the time of his illness, saved the family from experiencing excruciating poverty and hardship. I will forever look at my brother John as my guardian angel who waded through fast-flowing rivers with me for the sake of pursuing my education, which at the time seemed far beyond reach. It's no secret that there has always been a special bond between myself and my brother John. I will always be indebted to my brother for his unselfish and dignified generosity.

I cared for and nursed my brother John when I briefly returned to Zambia in 2011.My mother had succumbed to early onset dementia, as outlined in my published book *Me and My Mum*, and I had returned to Zambia to care for her. My brother had chronic heart problems, but despite much bureaucracy at the Zambian Ministry of Health, I managed to secure my brother's passage to India under a government initiative where he had a pacemaker fitted. Unfortunately, despite the successful heart surgery, my brother passed away in February 2013, two months after receiving his treatment in India. I still miss him terribly. Not a day passes without me thinking about him. He would have provided a wealth of information about Grandad, just as he did when I was writing my first book. MHSRIP

The Scary Encounter with Lumpa Cult Followers

Once in a lifetime one finds oneself in the wrong place at the wrong time. My first mishap involved a scary encounter with a religious cult on my way home from Chipili Girls' Boarding School. It had been reported that the cult followers were kidnapping people as they fled from conflict with government soldiers in Chinsali, Northern Province, now known as Muchinga Province in North East Zambia.

Just after Zambia's independence in 1964, there was an uprising between political cadres and the followers of a religious cult led by a certain Alice Mulenga Lenshina. This

Christian cult originated in the Chinsali district and spread rapidly to surrounding areas.

According to an account from archived Zambian newspapers, Alice Mulenga Lenshina lived from 1924 to 1978. It is reported that in 1953 Alice became seriously ill when she suffered from cerebral malaria which put her into a coma for three days. However, when Lenshina woke up, she testified to the people that whilst in her coma trance, she had received spiritual instructions to start a church. Lenshina started a religious movement called the Lumpa Church. According to writers' accounts, the movement was anti-witchcraft and opposed to adulterous practices. Its followers were requested to surrender various traditional and tribal artefacts, and all witchcraft paraphernalia was to be discarded in specially allocated and secured huts.

Various writers have testified that there was considerable improvement in the moral and social standards of people in the districts where the cult operated. However, certain beliefs of the Lumpa Church (such as drinking their own urine and asking followers to fly from treetops) caused anxiety and raised the suspicions of politicians, and soon there were conflicts between political groups such as The United National Independence Party and the Lumpa cult followers.

Unfortunately, things took a nasty turn, and there were stories of torture and dreadful massacres of members of the Lumpa Church. The fighting accelerated to a point where the government had to intervene by sending in combat soldiers who killed hundreds of cult followers and also lost some of their own soldiers in the process. In August 1964, the Lumpa Church was banned in Zambia and followers who survived the massacre ran to Zaire where they were granted asylum. Lenshina and her husband were arrested and sent to prison where they spent the rest of their lives. Her husband died first and Lenshina passed away fourteen years later.

It so happened that the escaping cult followers were using the same route from the Northern Province through to Zaire as we schoolchildren were. I was in the area on that particular day when Lumpa members were travelling along the Kasama/ Luwingu road via Chipili and Mansa en route to Zaire.

The rumour that Lumpa cult followers were passing through that night spread like wildfire. Stranded with a group of five or six of my fellow pupils on a road junction where we were waiting for a connecting bus to take us home, we found ourselves gripped with enormous anticipation and fear of the advancing menacing cult. Villagers at the junction warned us that we might get kidnapped and raped or killed. We had often found the villagers at Mano junction to be very unpredictable; sometimes they showed no mercy to the travelling public, including schoolchildren such as us, travelling to and from school. However, they were kind enough to warn us not to spend a night in the open air as we usually did. They would often advise us to make a fire and wait there until the arrival of our bus the following day.

On this particular day, however, it was different. We didn't know what to do as we had nowhere safe and secure to sleep. One of the girls in the group, the daughter of a teacher at our village school, suggested that we walk to the next village where her grandparents lived. We started off on foot, half-walking, half-running. Despite the fact that we were all less than thirteen years old, we quickly covered the five- or six-mile distance between the two villages. Ruth Sule's grandparents welcomed us and were pleased and relieved that we had made such a wise decision, as their village had also been warned about the arrival of the dangerous Lumpa cult followers.

Just before sunset, we saw a large group of about fifty men, women and children, all dressed in long white robes, walking through the village asking for the headman's house. The women and the girls wore white scarves on their heads. Nervously, we all came out to watch them. There were rumours that Lumpa cult members travelled at night or late evening, probably for fear of being apprehended by police or soldiers, and that when they reached a village, some would hide on the outskirts, waiting to find out what kind of reception the advance group received. If villagers became hostile to the advance group, it was said that the sect members would attack the village from both fronts. There were also reports of women and children being kidnapped from defeated villages. Hence the cult's unpredictable behaviour frightened villagers all along their chosen route.

I was surprised to see that the men in the group had their hair in cane row plaits. I thought that was strange because in my village men did not plait their hair. It would have been frowned upon. Of course, little did I know that fashions would change and that men nowadays plait their hair in cane rows, or cornrows, the world over. This style has been made fashionable today, even in the Western world, by professional role models such as footballers and actors, musicians and people in the fashion world, as well as trendy young lads. For me personally, I still find it amazing that such a practice, which was scorned and shunned by the society I grew up in, could have become so fashionable.

Adults and children in the village watched in bewilderment as droves of strange-looking people swamped their village. However, the village headman was very diplomatic. He welcomed the group and gave them food and water. He offered them a house where they could spend a night. Strangely, the group declined the offer of shelter. Instead they requested hot water so that their women and children could bathe and promised to leave the village thereafter. The village headman quickly organised the requested baths – probably hoping that the group would soon depart from his village if he obliged with their demands.

And as promised, calmly and slowly, the group walked away with women carrying babies on their backs and men carrying food and water. Watching them walk away, it seemed like a group of proud peacocks flying away from their nests. It was a spectacular scene. Little as I was, I wondered how such peaceful, humble and gracious-looking people could be involved in kidnapping and harassing people, let alone engaging in fierce fighting with armed forces. Were the rumours about them nothing but political propaganda? Or not – I was too young to think of wolves dressed in sheep's clothing. These were men and women battling against and even killing armed soldiers. How they did it, only God knows.

After their departure, the village remained silent for a good two or three hours. I suspect the village headman had sent out his spies who might have reported back that the cult members had indeed moved on to the next village. Remember, there were no telephones, let alone mobile phones in the area at that time, and spying was the only way of finding out what was happening within the vicinity of a village. After what seemed like 'waiting from hell' the village headman announced that it seemed the village was safe and that the Lumpa followers had indeed moved on to the next village However, everybody was advised to keep guard and not to allow women or children to venture outside.

Nothing happened throughout that night and I and my fellow pupils walked back to Mano junction, got on our bus and travelled safely home the following day.

Up to the present day, I have not heard what happened to the exiled Lumpa cult followers. Politics in Africa have always been obnoxious, edgy, volatile, deadly and unstable; one has to tread carefully before dipping one's fingers into boiling water. It is best to remember that 'curiosity killed the cat'.

It goes without saying that those were events from my Chipili days – some periods are not worth remembering. They are best locked up in our metaphorical boxes and forgotten!

CHAPTER SEVENTEEN

MY FATHER

According to an account given to me by my late elder brother John Jairous Chama, my father, known as Mr Jairous Chama Katebe was born around 1919 at Kabwela Village, Chief Mulala situated on Mwampanda River in the Northern Province of Zambia.

Growing UP Without a Father

My brother informed me that our grandfather was called Jam Bwalya and nicknamed by friends as Sixpence Mwendeulu Bwalya. He was one of the recruits sent to fight the Germans in East Africa during the First World War in 1918/19 and he perished there. My father did not see or know his father as Bwalya went to war when his wife (our paternal Grandma Kapungwe) was in her early stages of pregnancy. The unborn child she was carrying was my father whom she named Chama Katebe. My father was denied the opportunity to know his father and to have a male role model in his life.

My father grew up under the watchful eye of his fiery, feisty, fast-speaking and ruthless mother Kapungwe (best known as Nakatebe Ofesi) meaning 'the mother of Katebe who is married to Mr Ofesi'. Grandma Kapungwe was a cunning and stubborn woman who stood up to men. When we were children, she told us that she had once single-handedly, armed with a small hoe *(malaba)*, chased lions which had invaded their village. After this incident, Grandma Kapungwe proclaimed herself village headperson, the title she was known by and which she only relinquished to her son (my father) many years later.

Zambian Recruits for
World War 1914–1919

In the Zambian archive papers, it is reported that some 20,000 Zambians were forcibly recruited as porters for the British forces in East Africa during the First World War and most of them perished of diseases or debilitation.

To think that one of those men was my grandfather Bwalya brings a sinking feeling into my entire body. This is a man who went to war, leaving his wife pregnant; he did not even have a chance of seeing or knowing his only son (my father) and today he is just a figure or a statistic. Any boy born on this earth, irrespective of their colour or creed, craves to know, emulate and grow under the watchful eye of his father. And yet my poor father was denied this liberty which most of us take for granted. It hurts even more to think that these men were forcibly recruited, and that they lost their lives in a war which they did not start, did not know, nor comprehend. To rub salt into the wound, my grandfather and others who perished in the war are described as war porters. They were denied the dignity of human rights in their lives and are further insulted in death by intimating that they were not good enough to be soldiers and fight in a war but instead were recruited to be 'war porters'.

It is also surprising that my father probably had the wrong perception of what his father went to do in East Africa. For example, my father portrayed to us (his children) the picture of his father going to fight in the war and he constantly referred to him as a war hero. He did not tell us that his father was a war porter. Those were brave men who might have handled guns after being trained to do so and to call them war porters is a racially motivated insult. Any credible reader will look at such reports with disgust before they make their own judgement and refer to them as undignified articles or books which are written with the full frills of colonial and imperialistic perspectives.

It is also humbling to know that when so many men were forcibly recruited for the war in East Africa, parts of Zambia were virtually depopulated of able-bodied men and that large tracts of fertile land, including the fine area where David Livingstone would have established his colony (the Serenje/ Mukushi farming belt), were taken by white settlers. According to the archives, more than 20,000 men were forcibly recruited to be war porters. The figure itself does not add up. How many British or German soldiers were there to have so many war porters? Which men fought the war? And why did recruited men perish in war if all they did was act as porters?

Unsung Political Hero

My father was this six-foot arrogant and very intelligent, competitive and self-taught gentleman who might have been amongst the cream of intellectuals at Zambia's independence in 1964, but missed the boat because of his humble beginnings, compounded by the lack of formal education.

My father was a political prisoner. He was sent to prison at Luwingu for three years from 1960-1963. His offence was that of being a ring-leader in burning the ill-fated identity cards (Icitupa), which ruling political parties had incited cadres all over the country to burn or throw away. My father came back from prison a more hardened politician and he boasted of how he had spent his time in prison helping in the kitchens as a chef. Despite his stint in prison, my father did not denounce his political activities and continued to lead the branch in his constituency up to Zambia's independence and thereafter. Our house was a hive of activity and was the meeting place for United Nations National Independence Party (UNIP) representatives travelling up and down the country. People in higher positions, some of whom were imprisoned with my father, ate and slept at our house. There were some men who came from Luwingu or Kasama; the likes of Mr Mike Mwamba who I hear is still alive and well. There were other prominent UNIP constituency or provincial representatives such as Mr Kaunda, Kani Kapya, Mr Kabaso, Mr Mbolela and many others whose names I cannot remember.

My father had a radio the size and shape of a big saucepan, from which he listened to news of his contemporaries being appointed to various positions after Zambia's independence in 1964. I remember as a child seeing many men come to our house to tune in and listen to the latest world news referred to in vernacular as 'Ilyashi Lya Umulabasa' or 'Lya Calo Chonse' meaning 'World News'. My father would sit there on a high chair explaining to other men what was being said and what it meant. I vividly remember one evening when he excitedly said that Mr Simon Mwansa Kapwepwe had been dressed in an official gown as Vice President or Vice Prime Minister. (Simon Mwansa Kapwepwe is one of Zambia's highly acclaimed politicians who rose to various high ranking posts after Zambia's independence in 1964.)

Later on in life, I learnt that admirers of Nkwame Kwame Nkrumah of Ghana, who was perceived as a role model for young African politicians, started to emulate his Ghanaian traditional men's wear. However, a few years later, the trend of politicians dressing in West African wrappers changed when the then President, Dr Kenneth David Kaunda resorted to wearing safari suits which others donned.

The point I am driving at is that my father, who lost his job with the Mine Police due to his political activities and later went to prison for his involvement in political unrest, which was rife in the country, has not been acknowledged or recognised by the Zambian government.

Did they (the Zambian government), at any point realise the kind of financial hardships some of us (children of unsung political heroes) suffered by having fathers as political prisoners whilst we were in boarding schools where authorities expected us to pay boarding school fees? What of the emotional stress and shame of being a prisoner's daughter? How does an eleven-year-old face a white missionary and say, sorry miss, I cannot afford to pay the £9.00 school boarding fees because my father is in prison? Somebody, somewhere, who may bother to read this book will reminisce and sum up what it meant to be innocent children or wives of Zambian unsung heroes. Has the shame and dire financial, psychological and social imperfection impacted on their adult lives?

Wheeling and Dealing

As stated earlier, my father was a self-taught African who grew up in a village but later carved himself a career as a mine policeman in Mufulira Mines. As a result of his political affiliations at Mufulira Mines, which witnessed the most effective strikes from miners, which in turn disrupted and weakened the colonial masters' grip on copper mining, my father and many other miners lost their jobs. With his father lost in the war, he had the full responsibility of looking after his mother and, after losing his job, he headed back home to go and look after his beloved mother.

My mother once told me how my father packed and loaded their cases full of what she perceived to be useless iron and steel tools. She said their luggage was so heavy that she decided to leave behind most of her own stuff. Those tools helped in setting up my father's various goldsmith ventures.

It is true that history repeats itself. Retrospectively, what happened to my mother in the late 1940s and early 1950s had to happen to me in the late 1970s. When my husband, who was sponsored to study accountancy in England in the early seventies, was recalled home in 1979, he selfishly filled cases with his accounting manuals and books and, in frustration, I decided to leave most household goods behind in the custody of good Zambian friends, hoping to send for them at a later date. Up to the present day I have never recovered the goods I left behind as I immediately lost contact with the very people who promised to keep my stuff and besides, we (my family) headed back to England after spending just three and half years in Zambia.

However, once back home, my father established his own village at which stage his mother relinquished her village headship to her beloved son. My father established himself as a village entrepreneur and ran various small businesses. He became a goldsmith using the big steel and iron tools he brought with him from the Copperbelt; he manufactured hoes, axes and many other essential small-scale agricultural tools. He became an area representative for the Bangweulu Cooperative, a business cooperation which bought agricultural produce at wholesale (beans, groundnuts, millet, maize, cassava) to be sold at outlets in Mansa, Copperbelt or any of the other bigger towns.

My father probably made his money by working as foreman for a white investor called George. Mr. George, as he was called, owned a prospectors' company which was mining manganese (hard, brittle, grey metal or its black oxide) in the area. It was by coincidence that manganese ore deposits were found just outside my father's compound, so a camp for workers was constructed on the outskirts of my father's village. There were a lot of new people coming to work for Mr George's company. Large heaps of gravel could be seen from far away as many shallow open pits sprang up. Business was booming in the area and our village turned into a small town with vehicles ferrying manganese deposits away nonstop, and people, some of them speaking unknown or new dialects, swamped the village.

My father ran a village store which served as a grocer shop, dress shop and supplied simple medicines and tablets such as caffeine, aspirins, quinine. He also had sewing machines where tailors made dresses, trousers and any other garments. He also owned many herds of cattle. It was rare for an Ushi man to be in possession of so many cattle.

He was also a big hunter who owned several guns and his white friends from the open pit used to come home and they would go out hunting together with big torches and guns at night. Our house was full of activity night and day. My father and his fellow hunters went hunting in Milundu forests which I hear is now a protected game reserve area.

My Father, the Religious Man

My father was an elder and leader in the Jehovah's Witness religion. All I can remember about this religious movement in which I was born is that my family attended Sunday Meetings and that our house was the centre of most activities. There were continual Bible studies and there were visitors or elders from sponsoring mother churches that stayed with us, hence our house served as a miniature headquarters for the movement.

Jehovah's Witnesses are well known for their strict discipline on moral issues and their converts' interpretation of the Bible, which sometimes renders members to break the law of the land. During the time I was growing up, in the 1960s in Zambia for example, some of the movement's principles displeased the ruling government. For example, some members forbade their children from singing the national anthem at school assemblies. This was contrary to both government and school regulations that expected every pupil to honour the country and its leaders by singing the national anthem. Hence the school authorities expelled the non-compliant. Unknown to the movement members at the time, their actions of withdrawing their children from school created a lack of highly educated individuals within the movement, and as a result, literacy became a big issue for Jehovah's Witnesses for many years as they could only provide basic education to expelled children.

Some of the Jehovah's Witnesses' diabolical principles continue to baffle the world, even from a modern day perspective. For example, the movement's negative views pertaining to blood transfusion paints an oblique picture on their beliefs and values.

Despite my father's high profile in the Jehovah's Witness movement, he did not forbid us (his children) from singing the national anthem. In fact, he foresaw the impending dangers and he personally gave instructions to us to ensure that we stood in front of the entire assembly and sang the national anthem loud and clear. I always wonder whether he gave the same advice to his fellow congregation members. At least my father had his children's interest at heart and when it came to making a choice between our education and his religious beliefs he chose wisely. After all, there is an old saying 'Give what belongs to Caesar to Caesar and what belongs to God to God'. A committed religious person does not interfere with politics. He prays and lets politicians rule the world.

As earlier stated, born to parents in the Jehovah's Witness religion meant being well disciplined. There are a lot of things I feel I missed out on in childhood as my father wouldn't allow us to indulge in certain activities which were being pursued by our peer groups. For this I thank my parents as their strict discipline paved the way to a well-balanced, disciplined adult life for most of us.

There were other positive aspects of growing up in my parents' religious movement. Families grow closer through Bible studies and children grow up in a loving, God-fearing environment. There is a lot of emphasis on acceptable discipline amongst children, and members treat other people's children like their own. I remember being very interested in baby-sitting for other members during church gatherings. I could swap babies from one to another and sometimes attempted to carry babies on my small back. My mother used to warn mothers about my flair for babies and I was under a watchful eye all the time.

However, when my father noticed my obsession with babies he started buying me dolls. My first doll was a wooden elephant which I carried on my back everywhere I went. Other proper girls' dolls followed. I suspect my father ordered them for me from his Oxendales mail order catalogue. I was so naughty that I remember using my father's towel to carry my baby elephant or any other doll if my mother refused to let me use one of her wrappers. Being Dad's golden girl, he never used to punish me for using his towel but I do not want to say or predict what would have happened if any sibling dared touch Dad's towel, let alone wrap a silly baby elephant in it.

The Immaculate Oxendales Suits

My father ordered his suits and other clothes from the Oxendales mail order catalogue, which sent his clothes from England. My brother John was always travelling to Mansa to pick up my father's ordered parcels. My father was then the best-dressed man I had ever seen in my life. He wore suits with white or blue striped shirts and square-patterned jumpers and socks. My father, who had a natural elegance about him, always stood out in a crowd. It was overwhelming to see him stand in front of everybody. He just had that authority and power about him. I used to feel so proud on the days that he came to my school because he dwarfed teachers and their suits looked like *'salaula suits'*, meaning second-hand clothes from charity shops, compared to my father's brand new suits from Oxendales. Indeed, my father was held in very high esteem by both teachers and ordinary people in his community.

Our Beautiful Thatched Bungalows

In those days, the sixties, my family lived a life of near luxury. We had a five- or six-bedroom, professionally thatched bungalow situated on a flattened ant hill. It had cement floors complete with bay windows. Although there was no electricity in the house, we had big paraffin lanterns which, when lit, were just as good as electricity. My family was not short of money or food and we surely led a privileged life which was admired and envied by many people in the area.

My Father the Disciplinarian and Visionary Enthusiast

To outsiders, my father might have been labelled as a tyrant. But to us, his family and children, he was just a strict disciplinarian who would not take "no" for an answer. He always wanted things to be done in a certain way. He also expected high standards of discipline. He never allowed us children to answer him back simply by shouting "Yes" or "Yes sir" *(Mukwa)*; he ordered all his children to answer him back "Yes Dad" (*Tata*). I must admit it was sometimes uncomfortable to say 'Tata' when he called you in front of other children, but my father did not give a damn and he would insist that you answer him properly before he let you go.

My father never expected any of his children to come home after an examination result at school in which one had fared badly. You did not tell my father your position in the class examination rating was number five. He would beat you and punish you accordingly. It was an open secret in our household that if you had not fared well in an exam, you simply told Dad that the results were not yet out. My father only accepted top of the class or second. We worked hard at it and things started coming naturally because we knew we had to pass with flying colours all the time.

Writing about my father's character today, I am convinced that he was a visionary enthusiast. There were times when he gathered the six of us (his children) together and started lecturing to us about a 'television set'. He talked about a wireless on which you could see people as they spoke. And out of the blue he pinpointed our various achievements in our adult lives. Up to the present day, my elder sister Jo accuses me of being my father's favourite because she remembers one occasion when my father said, "You, Bupe, will live in a faraway land and you will be driving cars like white women do." In puzzlement, all of us laughed and I remember protesting to what Dad had just said by jokingly hitting back at him with both hands for singling me out and embarrassing me in front of everybody. My father just looked at me and laughed his head off.

My younger brother was very difficult as a child. But this is the boy to whom my father had given his own father's name, Bwalya, and my father desperately wanted him to be educated. He would drag him out from under the bed where he would be hiding to avoid going to school, and would beat him up until my brother agreed to go to school with the rest of us. We used to hate our brother's behaviour because it meant all of us would be late for classes because of him.

It surprised the family that the culprit pulled up his socks and ended up working for the mines as an electronics engineer. He has even progressed to become a lecturer at university level. I am sure my little brother is not even aware of his childhood misdemeanors.

Unfortunately, my father suffered a premature death. He died on 5th October 1973 and, just like his father, he did not live long enough to reap the rewards of his hard work in educating his children. In Africa, giving proper education to one's own children is a disputed unconditional life insurance. All the same, we (his children) will continue to carry the banner of his encouragement and goodwill to pave the way to our future destinies.

If my father was alive today, he would say to me, "Bupe, what did I tell you? You live abroad and you drive, but one thing you should remember is that if you are given a job or assignment to do, make sure you do it properly."

I feel my father has approved of what I do and would be proud to know that I have written this book. I must confess I have felt his presence from the beginning of this project up to the end. There were times when I thought about giving up on writing the book, and then out of the blue I would start thinking of my father and how disappointed he would be at my failure. Then fresh, positive ideas would start flowing into my head and within hours I would be back on my laptop typing furiously as though the new ideas would evaporate in the air if I delayed putting them on paper. It is with such deep feelings of gratitude that I have decided to dedicate this book to my father and grandparents whose wise and loving guidance I dearly and honestly miss!

Auntie Silica was my father's youngest half-sister. My paternal grandmother Kapungwe was a no-nonsense woman. She changed husbands as she wished. From what I was told, she married men from the same clan, hence all her children belonged to the Balumbu Clan –I am not sure about her first marriage where she had Uncle Chotwe Miyambo, her first son.

Legend has it that Uncle Miyambo was later recruited to fight in the Second World War in Burma for the British Army. All I can remember about him is that he had lost a finger on one of his hands in the war for which he used to draw a war pension at Mansa Boma. I vividly remember how, as a child, I used to refuse to shake his hand, probably because one finger was missing. He took it so well although he used to tease me over it and address me as "the little one who is afraid of shaking my hand" or something like that – just innocent, childish, fearful imaginations and anxieties on my part.

Grandma Kapungwe's second marriage was to Bwalya Mwandeulu who was recruited to join the British Army fighting against the Germans in the First World War in East Africa.

According to Tim Lambert's report, Zambia, or Northern Rhodesia as it was called, suffered severely in World War I. *(A Short History of Zambia)* Approximately 3,500 Zambians were recruited to fight the Germans in Tanzania, then a German colony. A further 50-10,000 Zambians were recruited by the British army as war porters. Even more disturbingly, a large amount of grain and cattle were impounded to be used by the military.

Before his recruitment into the army, Bwalya had one daughter, Chishala, with Grandma Kapungwe. However, as previously mentioned, Grandma was a few months pregnant with my father when Bwalya left to join the British army in East Africa. Bwalya perished in the war and never returned home; hence he did not see his son. Surprisingly, and against all odds, my father used to boast about his war hero father and he never had any bitter feelings against the war which took his father away from him. To Dad, his father was a brave soldier who died fighting and nothing less. I suspect that, at times, my father used to think that he inherited his shooting and hunting instincts from his soldier father! No wonder he worked as a mine policeman. My father loved to be in charge, the chief commander, the organiser, achiever, moderator, giver and the chief hunter of wealth, religion and food to feed the masses. He used to tell me, young as I was, that losing a father since birth meant he had to grow up overnight to become the man of the house, and that he took his responsibilities very seriously from a very young age.

Having said that, Grandma Kapungwe got remarried, to Mr Ofesi, another man from the same Balumbu clan and had two daughters with him. My father doted on his half half-sisters Sophia and Silica, whom he cared for tirelessly, despite the fact that they both married. I do not remember seeing or knowing Auntie Sophia, who must have died as a young mother, leaving two daughters who were brought up by Grandma Kapungwe and Auntie Silica. I knew my cousins Anis and Katebe (Auntie Sophia's daughters) who should still be alive somewhere in Zambia. Oddly enough, my father cared for his stepfather, Mr Ofesi, despite the fact that Grandma Kapungwe became fed up with him and later divorced him.

As a child I was surprised that Grandma Kapungwe had her own house and that Grandpa Ofesi lived in a separate house, but at the same time I could not understand why Grandad Mulutula and Grandma Lucie Mulala lived in the same house at Katobole village. Each time I asked my mother about my paternal grandparents' living arrangements, my mother, who did not seem to like her fierce and forceful mother-in-law, would jokingly say, "Your grandma finds things wrong in all the men she marries." I could not understand what Mum meant, but she would shut me up and say, "Ofesi is a good man; it is just that woman who finds faults in every person near her." Our discussion would end there and I would not ask any further questions thereafter. As can be expected, my mum and Auntie Silica cooked and provided meals for Mr Ofesi.

As mentioned previously, Grandma Kapungwe once told us children a story of how she chased lions which had invaded their village while the men froze in fear and would not leave their houses. She said some men hid under their improvised beds while others who tried to come out failed as they thrashed both legs in one shorts/ trouser leg and fell down! Grandma picked up a small hoe *(ka malaba)* and came out of her house. She made some deafening and threatening noises whilst charging towards the roaring lions. She waved her small hoe violently, calling on all her dead ancestors to help her chase the beasts from the village. She cursed the enraged lions at the top of her voice and suddenly she saw them running away towards a nearby stream. She chased them across the river then she returned home and proclaimed herself the 'village headman'. She told the cowardly men of the village that she could no longer be ruled by wimps of men who wet themselves at the sound of advancing roaring lions. And from that day, she became the village headman. She only relinquished her title and powers to her beloved and youngest son, my father, whom she commanded to give up his policeman job on the Copperbelt to come and head her village when she felt and realised that she could no longer carry on with the task. That was Grandma, always in charge of things (*mwabombeni mama*). Well done, Grandma, for introducing me to'girl power' at such an early age.

That is the kind of bravery Grandma Kapungwe possessed. She also had a sharp tongue and could easily and squarely cut down any rebellion and would trash anybody who tried or dared to stand up to her, man or woman. Well done, Bana Katebe Ofesi! Your genes must have been passed on to some of your fortunate offspring – not me though! Having said that, I laugh at jokes thrown at me by my own siblings who possess that dry sense of humour. Each time I visit Zambia, they make jokes about 'Na Katebe Ofesi' (the mother of Katebe) – that is how Grandma Kapungwe was addressed after her beloved son, my father, and nobody else. It was like, "Here comes Na Katebe Ofesi" or "Be careful of what you are saying, Na Katebe Ofesi is in Town!" Not bad for Bupe, whom Grandma Kapungwe did not even acknowledge as she, Grandma, dismissed me as a father's child who had been brainwashed by teachers at school! Sometimes she was very spiteful towards me and would tease my parents, especially my mother, and she would sarcastically say things like, "Ooh, that Bupe will never have any children because she has spent all her fertile childbearing years at school. By the time she finds a man to marry her, she will be too old for childbearing!" I quite agree with the saying 'Be careful with what you wish for.' It was my cousin whose mother and grandmother never allowed her to go to school who has turned out to be childless in adulthood, constantly widowed and leading a life in dire straits. You see, Grandma! Here, I am! Can you see me, wherever you are, among the stars, up there! It is me, Bupe, whom you had written off, who is today writing and singing your praises! Thank God I was too young to internalise those vicious utterances from my paternal grandmother. I only came to hear about them when I was researching what people knew about my relationship with my paternal side of the family.

Auntie Silica was the youngest and favourite of my father's three surviving sisters, hence my closeness to her daughter Jenny who was my best friend and cousin all rolled into one. My father usually would not allow me to play with any child who did not attend school. However, being an only child, Auntie Silica wouldn't allow Jenny to attend school as she wanted her daughter to marry early and produce a lot of grandchildren for her. Although Jenny started marrying early, and like her grandmother divorced many husbands, and also suffered multiple widowhood, she sadly did not have any children from any of her marriages. On the other hand, my father pushed me further and further into education which meant spending my entire teenage years trotting from one boarding school to another.

On reflection, I feel sorry for my dear friend and cousin, especially since Auntie Silica died many years ago, leaving her daughter on her own. Jenny now is a staunch Christian and still lives at Mansa – the provincial headquarters for Luapula Province of Zambia. Each time I visit Mansa, I make sure she comes over and we end up having a good laugh, talking about all those childhood stories in my hotel room. She still remains my childhood best friend, and I am happy that she seems content in her own way. She tells me she has many friends, mostly from church, so I hope what she tells me is true and I always include her in my quiet prayers.

With hindsight, Jenny is a good girl. She often asks about my children and grandchildren about whom I do not usually feel free to talk in her presence. She is often inquisitive about their looks and what language they speak. I tell her they probably resemble me and their father as we are their parents and that they speak English. This tickles Jenny as she cannot understand why anybody who is not white European cannot speak Bemba or Nyanja (popular Zambian dialects). I tell her they have lived and grown up in England, hence they speak the English language. Then she goes on asking about the food they like or eat until I distract her with another question or joke about an old village secret or another humorous village story, both of which she would start telling me whilst in fits of laughter – oh dear! During those times we both go back down memory lane and just talk about our childhood experiences.

Going back to my childhood days, Jenny was slightly more mature than I was. The fact is that she did not go to school and was 'a spoilt only child'. She seemed to talk about traditional adult things with her mother and grandma. Writing about it now, it seems to me that Jenny was embroiled into a lot of adult gossip. She always knew about whatever was happening in the village. At the time, I would envy her for not going to school and I constantly complained to my mother as I thought Jenny was given VIP treatment. My mother would just laugh and urge me to get on with my schooling. However, the fact that Auntie Silica did not allow Jenny to go to school caused a lot of friction between her and my father who wanted to put his children's education first. Thank you, Dad, and well done (*Twatotela ba Tata*). Instead of school, Jenny was instilled with all traditional values, customs and beliefs. I was quite naïve at the time and could not understand some of the things she said to me, and each time I consulted my mother on such issues I got a beating for even uttering such words or sentences which were beyond my age and were reserved for adults only.

Sadly my cousin Jenny passed away on 25th February 2021. I will miss her dearly. Each time I visit Zambia I took clothes and give her money. I financed her funeral by sending sending enough money for her funeral. MHSRIP

CHAPTER EIGHTEEN

THE CURSE OF THE KATAMBALA FAMILY

As one might expect, Jenny frightened the hell out of me when she confided in me about the curse of the Katambala family who had just arrived to settle in our village. To me it appeared that this strange family came from very far away and had settled near our village. The family included Mr Katambala himself, a very short, dark-skinned man with shifty, sunken eyes. He did not speak to any children or adults in the village. The few times I caught a glimpse of Mr Katambala were only when and if he was summoned by my father to appraise him of certain issues.

On those occasions, Mr Katambala would approach our house without any sound as his furtive movements were executed with devious quick steps, usually taken with precise haste. He would greet my father with tightly zipped lips – just a little sound would escape his lips but then he would bend double, stretching his hand to greet my father. This was probably his way of showing respect to people in power, especially my father who commanded respect from everyone, regardless of their seniority in the area. And my father, who was a tall, authoritative figure, would point to a chair without saying a word in acknowledgement of Mr Katambala and, like an obedient child, Mr Katambala would perch himself, looking frightened, on the edge of the chair with his feet barely touching the ground. Looking at Mr Katambala appearing so frightened and vulnerable in my father's presence, I always wondered what on earth such a man could discuss with my father.

At this point I would run out of the room, half-choking on tears, as I would be so disappointed and angry that Mr Katambala did not even acknowledge my presence. Usually, adults who came to our house would shower me with praises before they even stretched out their hands to greet my father. They usually commented on how tall I had grown or how quickly I was turning into this beautiful woman. They would say anything pleasant about me, probably to appease my father, or it would have been their clever way of breaking the ice with my authoritative father, who they knew doted on me so much. And my father would be holding my hand as though showing me off to frightened visitors. He would smile at me and then gently let go of my hand and ask me to retreat to the veranda or kitchen where my mother and other siblings would be waiting for me with one hundred questions like: "Who is with Dad?" "What did they bring with them?" Or, "What did they say to you?" In those days, it seemed to me that everybody respected my father to a certain extent. It appeared as though they were petrified of him, and when he summoned them to our house they would come in, shaking like a leaf, and expecting the worst from him, and yet sometimes he just wanted to enquire about their own health and that of their families.

In contrast, Mr Katambala's wife, Auntie Maria, was an extremely beautiful woman. She had very fair skin pigmentation and could easily be mistaken for a mixed-race woman. She also had a nice well-built body, a very nice figure, and an infectious smile. Her high-pitched laughter could pierce the sky above and bring joy and happiness to her audience. She always stopped to have a short chat with my mother, and the two women would share a joke or two before this sharp, high-pitched sound would puncture the air, breaking the deadly silence of morning blues and instead injecting the calm blue skies with warmth and tranquility. Oh God, the sound of Auntie Maria's laugh spread like fire and brought smiles to other people's faces. Young as I was, I sometimes over overheard big boys and adult men making comments on her beauty, despite the fact that she was totally blind. Her beauty completely masked her visual impairment.

However, most women in the village were envious of Auntie Maria's beauty and shunned her. Some women were so cruel and turned to various devious ways of torturing her by directly reminding her that she was blind. Some would say nasty things to her like, "If only you could see, you would have taken over all our men who are besotted with your infectious laughter." The more outrageous ones would go as far as saying to her things like, "Why do you laugh like that? Not everybody wants to have their eardrums pierced by your high-pitched laugh." Such comments made Auntie Maria sad, but my mother loved her and always protected her. I witnessed a couple of occasions when my mother told off whoever directly referred to Auntie Maria's disability or made rude comments or remarks about her in my mother's presence.

Auntie Maria and her husband had one daughter who was an only child. Emma was her mother's guide. As earlier mentioned, in Africa, in those days and even now, there are no facilities like white canes or guide dogs for blind people. In Zambia it is normal for blind adults to rely on their children to guide them around all the time.

Emma did not inherit the angelic looks of her mother. She had taken on her father's dark skin and muscular, dwarf-like features, complete with his small sunken eyes, however she possessed her own beauty and aura. It goes without saying that 'beauty is in the eyes of the beholder'. Emma was a very special girl and a God-given gift to her family. Young as she was, Emma ignored everything around her and just concentrated on caring for her disabled mother. Because of her caring responsibilities, Emma was unable to go to school like any other child. She also endured many other sacrifices like not playing with her peers and having to listen to all the comments and insults directed at her parents by cruel villagers. To many people, she just had sturdy, boyish looks and wore strange oversized clothes which made her appear odd, fierce, unfriendly and strange. There was no childish innocence about Emma and all of us children were scared of her. She never tried to make friends with either children or adults. Probably as a result of her mother's disability and dependence, Emma had instinctively matured beyond her age. She behaved like a grown-up and yet she was barely a little girl, burdened with insurmountable responsibilities. I used to feel sorry for her and I constantly asked my mother why Emma did not play with other children My mother would just look at me and say, "Emma has a lot of things to do and therefore has no time to waste in being playful."

With all due respect and considering the fact that the Katambala family had just moved into the area, they seemed not to have enough food nor any essentials of their own. They used to do a lot of work for others in exchange for food and clothing, hence their status in the village was dented enormously.

In our village in those days, for example, buying things using hard cash was rare. Cash transactions were only reserved for buying new clothes or any other manufactured commodities, mostly in my father's village store. Other deals were struck by exchanging certain goods for food stuffs. Poorer families worked for those with plenty in exchange for food or even clothing. I remember having a lot of people carrying out various domestic chores at our house in exchange for food, clothing or simple tablets for malaria and headaches. This is how I came to know Auntie Maria and Emma Katambala as they usually carried out errands for my mother in exchange for food and clothing.

Each time the duo left their house, Maria held onto Emma who led the way to wherever they were going. However, in the eyes of a little girl, the duo resembled a military marching parade. For example, the mother had wider strides and Emma had to keep up with her mother's steps, hence the duo seemed to be in a hurry all the time as they marched on. Their walkabout included going to draw water from the well, going to the fields or walking about in the village. It used to puzzle me to see an adult holding on to a young girl all the time. I used to stare at them until they faded out of my sight.

Late one afternoon I dashed out of our house, jumping off the veranda two steps at a time. My destination was Jenny's house; she had promised to show me something. I really wanted to find out what she had to show me. As I crossed a T-junction road, which led to the well, I saw Emma and her mother marching along from the opposite direction. I wanted to cross over so I could avoid them. Within seconds, I heard Auntie Maria call my name. I turned round and wondered how she knew it was me. I answered, "Yes Auntie." Auntie Maria said, "Bupe, where are you going?"

I felt frightened and stood still as though fixed in a trance. Thinking of an answer, I stammered and managed to whisper out some rather in audible words: "I am not going anywhere."

Auntie Maria said, "Come with us to the well." I looked up at Emma and noticed that she was glaring at me in a menacing way, probably envying me for my freedom which she never had. She looked me up and down and then turned and pulled her mother, instinctively urging her to move. The duo strode on with their usual marching movements. I stood there still wondering how Auntie Maria had guessed it was me running away from them and why Emma frightened me so much.

I was still standing there not knowing what to do when Jenny appeared from nowhere and pushed me forward. She then held my hand and started running. I was protesting at her speed and kept asking what she was doing, but she would not let go of my hand until we reached her house.

Jenny looked at her mother apologetically and said, "Mother, I found her talking to them."

Her mother said, "To whom?"

Jenny said, "To the two witches, Emma and her mother."

I saw fear in Auntie Silica's face and half-questioning and half-accusing me she turned to me, and said, "Haven't your parents warned you about the Katambala family?"

Half-crying and partly panicking, I said, "No, no, no."

Then Auntie paused and asked, "What did they tell you?"

I said Auntie Maria asked me to go to the well with them.

"Oh, my God," Auntie Silica sighed. "What is that woman up to?" Turning to me, she said, "You must be very careful and next time do not talk to those people when you see them. You run away, you hear me?"

I answered, "Yes Auntie."

A few minutes later, Jenny and I were rolling in dirt outside the house, laughing at nothing and everything. A few minutes later we decided to go and play mums to our wooden dolls. As though Jenny had just remembered something, she sat me down and said, "Didn't you know that Emma and her mother Maria are witches? That is why they have come to settle here where nobody knows them. And because they are witches, that is why the mother is blind." And then Jenny continued, "The people Maria bewitched came and gouged out her eyes in the night." At that point, I became petrified and I stood up, trembling from head to toe. I did not want to hear anymore of Jenny's utterances; I must have been scared to death to think that I had just been talking to two witches. I gathered courage and told Jenny that I wanted to go back home. Jenny said, "Wait a minute, I have not finished telling you what my mother told me."

I said, "What?"

Jenny said her mother and grandmother had told her that any child who shakes hands with Mr Katambala or his wife or daughter may dream of them at night and eventually die in their sleep.

At that point, I panicked and went into a trance; I eventually gave one big wail and ran off in the direction of our house. As I ran home, all I could think of or see was Emma and her mother. I started planning my escape from sudden death in my sleep. At last, I decided that I would not go to sleep at all that night as I was sure I would dream about the Katambala family and die in my sleep. All the same I wanted to keep what Jenny had told me a secret as she had warned me not to tell anybody.

I tried all the tricks I knew which could keep me awake but, alas, I did not even realise that I was slowly drifting into a deep sleep. Within minutes, I saw those images – oooh, no, no, it is Emma, Auntie Maria and Mr Katambala beckoning to me! As though in slow motion, Emma was beckoning to me to follow her. She never spoke but just stretched her hand to me. I desperately cried, "No, no, no," and started running away and the next minute my mother was standing over me asking why I was screaming in my sleep. I woke up sweating and panting and I decided to tell her what I had been told earlier in the day and I also told her about my dream.

My mother, who could not stand any nonsense, looked at me and said, "Get up, and sit up, and by the way, what were you doing with Jenny? And who told her Maria and Emma were witches?" Then she said, "Next time you say such nonsense things to me I will beat you up, now go back to sleep and stop being a nuisance."

"Yes Mum," I said and went back to sleep, but could still see the images of Emma and her father. I closed my eyes tightly and prayed to God Almighty that those images would leave me alone. I must have fallen asleep because I was awoken by sounds of laughter. My mother would have been telling my siblings about what I had told her the previous night. I pretended not to be awake because I was embarrassed and most of all I was afraid of the teasing I was going to get from my sisters and brothers. And most of all, I was scared that my mother would tell Auntie Silica. I dreaded to think that the information would be passed on to my father. I would be told off and the worst-case scenario would be getting a good beating for saying such things about another family. My father expected his children to be the most obedient and well-behaved ones in the entire village. We were not expected to tell lies or say bad things about anybody. We were in most cases not allowed to mix and play with other children in the village because my parents thought that other children were so deviant and devious to the extent that their bad behaviour would impact on us.

However, when I finally dragged myself out of bed, my mother called me and sat me down. She surprised me, because I was expecting a good beating, but instead she said softly to me, "Don't listen to what people say. They do not mean what they say; some people are suspicious and superstitious and others just do not like new people in the village. Maria is a very nice person. The fact that she is blind does not make her a witch." As though talking to a fellow adult, she continued, "Mr Katambala had a falling out with his brothers in the village where he lived, hence he has come over here, bringing along his family to get some protection from your father." And as though warning me, my mother said, "Jenny is a young girl and should not be saying such bad things about other families." Then she said, "I will have a word with her mother later in the day."

At that point, I cried out, "No, no, Mum please, do not speak to Auntie Silica about it, I was just lying; Jenny and her mother did not say anything to me. Please, please Mum do not say anything to them or you will get me in trouble," I pleaded and sobbed.

My mother then turned to me and said, "Did you make up that story and the screaming in your sleep?"

I answered back and said, "Yes."

My mother snapped, "What?"

Through tears I said, "Yes, yes, yes – oh, no, no."

My mother would have been surprised herself because, half-laughing, and at the same time trying to appear serious and stern with me, she said, "Do you realise that telling lies is a sin?"

I said, "Yes, yes, yes."

My mother then asked, "Were you telling lies when you told me what Jenny said to you?"

I said, "No, no, no."

This yes, yes, yes and no, no, no, went on and on until my mother got fed up and warned me against making such allegations about people and I must have been grounded for a couple of hours. I was punished and reprimanded against going out and coming back home with rubbish foolish stories.

However, my brothers and sisters took pity on me and kept me company and played with me inside the house, all the time pretending to be reading the Bible as it was one of the imposed conditions attached to my curfew. We did that at the top of our voices each time we heard Dad's or Mum's footsteps and yet we were actually playing hide and seek the whole time. A few hours later, the curfew was lifted and I was free once more to roam about the entire village, while avoiding Jenny and her mother's house at all costs.

On reflection, whilst writing this book, I saw a documentary on British television about child carers and I instinctively thought of Emma and her mother, Auntie Maria. I wondered what had happened to them. Are they still alive? Have they moved somewhere else? Did Emma marry and find some happiness? What would have happened to her mother if Emma had married and moved on with her life? I just went on and on imagining what might have become of the Katambala family until I realised that the only way I will put their ghosts to rest is to write about them. I actually psyched myself up and thought, "I am now an adult, and even if I dream about them I won't die in my sleep as per Jenny's childish advice."

Incidentally, the more I think about the Katambala family, the more I start feeling guilty for not being of assistance to them when they came to live in our village. Could I have done things differently to assist Emma? But then, I was just a small girl as well and most of the time I was away at boarding schools. I completely forgot about the Katambala family as I left the village to pursue my studies far and beyond our village limits. How on earth could I justify the hostility Auntie Maria and Emma received from jealous female villagers? How can one start to apologise on behalf of all the children and adults who scorned the Katambala family? Admittedly, I have just resolved that the Katambala family saga is a typical example of the communal baggage which one must carry on behalf of the community.

It is difficult to explain, but having spent so much time in boarding schools then moving to a big city, getting married and migrating abroad, I cannot remember the whereabouts of all the people I knew in my childhood. I had completely forgotten about the Katambala family until I saw the documentary.

However, simply dedicating the entire chapter to the Katambala family is a true testimony that I am singing their praises and I feel they are very special to me, in that they still occupy a small portion of my subconscious after all these years.

CHAPTER NINETEEN

SHINING A SMALL TORCH DOWN MEMORY LANE

Whilst writing this book, I attended a church service on Sunday, 27th December 2015 at Belle Vue Baptist Church, Southend-On-Sea, Essex. It was something I looked forward to as the following day, 28th December, was my birthday. I wanted to cleanse all the ill feelings and uncertainties of 2015 and start 2016 on a renewed fresh spiritual plane.

Sitting there listening to the preacher, it dawned on me that I had walked through life without reflecting on where I had come from or thinking about the wonderful adventurous childhood I was exposed to in an African village. I also thought of how I had started writing stories about my grandad but then stopped and put them away and they had remained untouched since 2006.

The service was lovely and the singing – mostly Christmas carols – took my breath away. It transformed me into this new purified little human being, full of kindness and forgiveness. When the female preacher of the day, Mrs Brenda Simms, asked the congregation to come forward and write something on sheets of A4 paper which she had strategically placed on tables lined up in the church's main aisle, I first of all hesitated, then I thought, I have a strong 'wish' which cannot wait until the New Year's Day resolutions! I stood up and gingerly walked to the table with many other worshippers, picked up the pen and wrote: "Dear Lord, let my husband, who has been in a coma since July 2015, wake up and say something to his children before you finally take him away from us." I signed the piece of paper, left it on the table and went back to my seat.

At first I shivered a little as I could not comprehend why I had come up with such a confession and wishful thinking when I had tried to be so strong and had never requested prayers nor talked with anybody at this church about my personal unfolding nightmare.

It all started on a Sunday morning, 5th July 2015, whilst attending a church service at Aveley Christian Fellowship Church in South Ockendon, Thurrock, where my second son lives. My daughter-in-law, who was running late, came to join me and whispered to me that something had happened to Dad. I asked what had happened to him. She said it appeared he had been attacked and was currently at Queen's Hospital, Romford and that Ken (my second son) was driving there now. I felt numb, but nothing prepared me for what I found on my arrival at Queen's Hospital. I was told that my husband had suffered brain damage following a fall or an attack and was in and out of consciousness. By this time, he could hardly converse with us. A few hours later he was put in an induced coma. Then came procedure after procedure to remove fluid from his swelling brain. A few weeks later, doctors told us that he was not responding to treatment and that they had failed to wake him up. And since then, he has remained in that comatose condition.

For me and our four children, our wish has been for him to tell us who did this to him or tell us what exactly happened to him. It has been a nightmare, sometimes too heavy to carry. Each time I look at any of my children's worried faces, I feel like bursting into a big scream, but if I did, who would be there to show strength and tenacity in a situation which has engulfed us without any warning signs?

Hence I wrote that little wish at church but I never thought about it when I left my house on that cold Sunday morning. Now seated back on my chair, I started worrying that people in the congregation might read what I had written and would stop me to talk about it. I had been attending services at this church for a couple of months as I had just relocated from my London home to Southend-on-Sea on the east coast. Whilst at church, I speak to one or two couples and Pastor Andy; other than that, nobody in the congregation knew that my husband was critically ill at Queen's Hospital London.

Then Mrs Simms, the preacher, came up with something which capsized my whole being and took me back into my childhood mode on which this book is based. Whilst preaching about the difference between light and darkness, she came up with a written passage which went as follows:

"There is a well-known piece of writing which says: 'In a dark, dark wood, there was a dark, dark house, and in that dark, dark house, there was a dark, dark room. And in that dark, dark room, there was a dark, dark cupboard and in that dark, dark cupboard, there was a dark, dark shelf. And on that dark, dark shelf, there was a dark, dark box and in that dark, dark box, there was...' and at this point we are left to decide what might be in the dark box. If it was me in that dark, dark room then in my dark, dark box, I would find a torch so that the darkness wasn't scary to me anymore, and I would be able to see my way back through the dark, dark room and the dark, dark house and the dark, dark wood by the light of my precious torch."

She continued and stated that, "It seems to me that light, even a little bit, will not only take away the darkness but will take away fear and give hope. It's odd how it works." (Sunday Sermon by Mrs. Brenda Simms, 27th December 2015.)

By the time the lady preacher finished the passage, I was in my own world, transported back into my childhood in which I have been engulfed since I started working on my latest book containing stories told to me whilst growing up at Grandad's Katobole village in north-east Zambia. I had, in my trance, gone back into my childhood and it felt like going back down memory lane.

CONCLUSION

I t is well documented that Dr David Livingstone depended on the courtesy and hospitality he received from his African hosts, whom he respected and treated more or less like equals, unlike the views held by his contemporary European explorers, that 'a negro' cannot improve beyond a certain point and would mentally remain 'a child'. Livingstone maintained that the African social habits and attitudes had a purpose and he sometimes felt that Africans were harmed, rather than helped, by European colonial attitudes and influence.

The 1,500 km journey, all undertaken on foot, was a gallant ordeal carried out by crossing swampy rivers, the natural habitat for crocodiles and snakes, sustaining unexplained tropical diseases, being threatened by attacks from tribal men and wild animals like lions and leopards. Livingstone's African porters marched on until they reached Bagamoyo in Tanganyika where they were paid meagre wages and summarily dismissed by Prideaux, the Assistant British Consul of the day.

Most written documents on Dr David Livingtone's African porters state that it is as though being dismissed unceremoniously was not enough for African porters. Even Jacob Wainwright, who accompanied Livingstone's coffin to England was treated badly and, in some stately homes, was resented for expressing certain mannerisms not expected of him as an African boy. But then Wainwright was taken away from his African culture at an early age and became accustomed to some middle-class values as taught to him by Europeans who brought him up. It is also said Susi and Chuma, who were sent for three months after Livingstone's funeral, were treated not as respected guests but were displayed at conferences dressed at the whim of their hosts for publicity purposes, hence their status became uncomfortably unclear. Were they nobles or savages? Were they honoured guests or servants? Were they paid or genuinely compensated for the work they did? Were they too, allowed to be explorers and discoverers of a strange and foreign land, or was that role exclusively preserved for white European men?

Dr David Livingstone's legacy:

"Had Dr Livingstone been a rationalist, he would have given up, a pragmatist, he would have abandoned his journeys, unambitious, he would not have spent his last years chasing the source of the Nile... He was an optimistic and obsessive idealist, who achieved his aim of opening a way into Africa for others" *(C.S. Nicholls).*

Long after Livingstone's death, missionaries from Scotland founded and opened Livingstonia Mission in Malawi where they started training African pastors to evangelise the Word of God in Malawi and surrounding countries – which had been Livingstone's dream.

As for the African descendants of Livingstone's African porters, they strongly feel that their ancestors were not adequately compensated by the British government. Despite a few medals given to a few senior porters like Susi and Chuma, there were seventy-nine dismissed porters who received nothing other than meagre wages given to them by Prideaux and they deserved more financial benefits and proper recognition.

This book has been written to show that there were other Africans who helped in the transportation of Dr David Livingstone's body from Zambia to Dar-Es-Salaam in May to October 1873.

Dr Livingstone's African servants in England

Despite the enormous task the African servants undertook, which some described as "a truly Herculean act, fit to be handsomely rewarded," Livingstone's African heroes were treated shabbily and disappeared into thin air without any compensation from the British government.

AFTERWORD
(ABOUT THE AUTHOR)

A gracious childhood and
an adventurous adulthood

Grace Chama-Pupe (née Grace Chama Katebe) spent her childhood at Katobole village, Chief Mulala, in Luwingu District, north-east Zambia. The village was headed by Grace's charismatic, authoritative and spin doctor grandfather, Mr Ngosa Shompolo Mulutula who narrated to her and his other grandchildren stories about his service to white colonial explorers which included his recruitment into the entourage of Dr David Livingstone's epic journey.

One of the most popular stories was his service as a pall bearer and porter in Dr David Livingstone's entourage which ferried the doctor's embalmed body from Chitambo near Serenje, Zambia, where he died, to Tanganyika (Tanzania) on the east coast of Africa for onward shipment on the Indian Ocean via Suez Canal to Great Britain. Grandad Mulutula also told us stories about his traditional healing talents, his magical powers to deal with witchcraft cleansers, his ability to down witch doctors who trespassed into his territory. (Unlike the British or Western beliefs of witch doctors riding a broom stick, the African beliefs are that witch doctors ride on human beings or use blood sucked from dead people as fuel, and when blood runs out the witch doctor drops down to the ground.) Grandad also talked about his inheritance practices and many other intriguing stories; some of them seemed to be riddles or fiction, although most were factual events.

To us children, all the stories seemed real and we took them very seriously. It felt like we were listening to stories being read from books. We got hooked and addicted on grand-fathers' stories as today's young generation's addition to computer games'.

Those stories narrated to me such a long time ago are very dear and meaningful to me and up to the present day are the focal point of my wellbeing and form the cornerstone of my destiny. For example, Grandad noticed and groomed my natural intelligence and tenacity in quick learning. He would purposely set me against older male cousins by dictating letters and asking us to read what we had written back to him, as well as reading letters he had received from his enlightened relatives, both activities which I did with ease whilst my older cousins couldn't even read nor write a word from Grandad's dictation.

At the age of eleven I was selected to attend the then prestigious Chipili Girls' Boarding School which was run by white Anglican missionaries. It was a good old school established in the 1940s/50s. Chipili Mission Boarding School for Boys and Girls near Mansa in Luapula Province has since produced many academics, politicians and clergy personnel in Zambia. Finally, I completed my secondary education at Kasama Girls' Secondary School in Northern Province where I obtained eight O-levels. This school too has produced serious politicians in Zambia such as cabinet ministers, permanent secretaries and a current female president of an opposition party; Ms Edith Nawakwi was my former school mate at Kasama Girls' Secondary School.

I enrolled for a secretarial course at Evelyn Hone College, Lusaka, Zambia and briefly held senior secretarial positions in the Zambian government which included secretarial assignments at United Nations Development Programme (UNDP) and Preference Trade Area (PTA) (now COMESA) in Zambia. I then emigrated to join my husband in the United Kingdom where I briefly undertook various temporary secretarial jobs which included a locally engaged staff assignment at Zambia High Commission in London.

Having experienced much frustration in secretarial jobs in England I decided to change my career and embarked on a four-year degree in social work at East London University and later enrolled at the University of Westminster where I obtained a Diploma in Community and Primary Health Care. I have worked in several London local authorities and the surrounding Home Counties as a social worker before finally relocating to Southend-On-Sea, in Essex.

After returning to England, following a two-year sabbatical break, during which time I cared for my ailing mother in Zambia, I started thinking of a career change once more. I started writing a book on my experiences with my mother, and when I returned home to the UK I continued undertaking temporary social work assignments to fulfil my financial obligations. I then started loving writing books, and I disengaged from practising social work. I now find myself introducing myself to people as an author and not a social worker.

I decided to relocate from London to Southend-On-Sea which provides me with a sea-front scenario which is a magnet for any writer. Since then my life has been transformed. I have found very good friends, mostly through the church, which comes with the unlimited spiritual love and growth for which I had been frantically searching. I am still very committed to my family in London and I am a permanent feature on road cameras on the A13 and A127 roads as hardly a few days pass by without me driving on those roads leading to London. I am very grateful to the Almighty God for guiding and placing me in a place (Southend-On-Sea) where I feel welcomed, safe, loved and mostly near to God.

Lately, I have realised that my choice of a social work pathway in Adult and Elderly Social Work Practice has manifested itself into a speciality of mental health conditions such as dementia. As fully outlined in my first published book, *Me & My Mum*, I have now embarked on running a charity on dementia awareness in UK Minorities and Third World countries with a special focus on Zambia. The charity's aims and objectives are:

To raise dementia awareness in UK minority communities;

To highlight the plight of dementia sufferers and their carers in Third World countries through educative literature, short films and well-organised and facilitated seminars/ workshops in both the UK and Zambia;

To fundraise for the establishment of dementia respite units for dementia sufferers and their carers attached to one or two hospitals in Zambia.

In addition, I registered a second charity called The Friends of Mansa General Hospital. This charity will assist in constructing a shelter, supplying beds, linen and equipment to carers who spend nights and days caring for inpatients at the hospital. Currently these people sleep on the floors in a neglected shelter without adequate sanitary or cooking facilities. I wish to co-ordinate this charity from the UK but eventually hand it over to committee participants in Zambia.

I find it difficult to convince my own people about the aims and objectives of the two charities. This reminds me of some of the challenging behaviours Jesus faced from his own people: "Doubtless you will quote to me this proverb, 'Doctor, cure yourself!'... and you will say, 'Do here also in your home town the things that we have heard you did at Capernaum.'"

And he said, "Truly I tell you, no prophet is accepted in the prophet's home town" (Luke 4: 20–24).

I find it hard not to spread the word on dementia awareness in Zambia where most people are embroiled in their cultural and traditional beliefs. They have their firm interpretation of dementia as madness or a disease suffered by people who practise witchcraft. The Zambian government has not highlighted dementia awareness and yet more emphasis is put on HIV and AIDS.

With hindsight, it is fair to say that I have had some very exciting opportunities as well as some drastic personal and professional failures in my life. On the positive side however, I had a very exciting childhood which I spent at my grandad's village where I had various values instilled in me, and which have been a cornerstone of my adult life.

Lastly, a Kenyan Writer Cecily Mwaniki once quoted Benjamin Franklin who stated that:

"If a man empties his purse into his head, no one can take it away from him. An investment in knowledge always pays the best interest." *(The Wisdom of Ages).*

GLOSSARY

Ndekulutula	I will hit you hard
Bwana Munali	Great Hunter (Dr Livingstone's African pet name
Bena fyalo	Foreigner
Ba mayo bana Chibwe	Auntie, the mother of Chibwe
Impemba	White clay – dug from river banks
Inswakala	White lime – probably made from powdered white marble
Imiti ikula, empanga	Children are tomorrow's future
Insaka	Village male communal shelter
Kapaso	African or native messenger
Impatishi	Protective thick socks
Cikabanga	Afrikaans language (Dutch)
Lozi	One of Zambian tribes/language
Nkula	Red powder made from ground tree bark
Nshima	Main Zambian meal made from maize flour, rice flour, cassava flour etc
Bana Chimbusa	Marriage Counsellors
Bena Mbulo	Steel Clan
Kalume Kepi	Short warrior or unperturbed Mabumba
Munshitina	brave short born leader
Kalume Kepi	Ceremonial name for brave shortleader
Cimambala	trickster, unreliable person

Impokeleshi	Bestowal bride
Mukolo	Senior Chief's Wife
Uluanga	Hare
CMML	Christian Mission in Many Lands
Chitokoloki	CMML mission station in North Western Province, Zambia
Nshila Newspaper	Vernacular local Newspaper
Mukolwe	Cockerel
Umunani	Relish
Ng'anda	House
Sandauni	Formal Village Party (Dancing from sun rise till dawn)
Mwashala yama	Brothers/uncles you are left behind and missing out on goodies (enticing sexual banter to raise stakes from male punters at Sandauni festival by Master of ceremony)
Moneni abanakashi	Look at these beautiful women dancers
abanaka imisana	withflexible spinning waists – Master of celebration banter)
Ba mobilo	Most feared non-compromising Mobile Unit
Iyee Mayo	Oh my God
Rumba Music	Franco/Lingala/Congolese music
Ilomba	Sea snake (Witchcraft charm) notorious for feeding on goat's milk, eggs and human foetuses' blood (as per Zambian beliefs)
Icitupa	Natives' Colonial idenity card
Ubutala	Maize storage barn

Mthunywa yi Nkosi	Southern Rhodesian African Messenger
Amacila	Hammock
Lumpa Church	Lenshina's Christian Cult
Nakatebe Ofesi	Mother of Katebe married to Mr Ofesi
Malaba	Small shoulder hoe carried by women for self-protection
UNIP	United National Independence Party
Ilyashi lya Mulabasa/ Ilyashi lya calo chonse	World News
Ushi	Tribe found around Mansa in Luapula Province, North East Zambia
Salaula	Second hand clothes
Mukwai	Yes Sir
Balumbu	Ushi Clan
Mwabombeni mama	Well done Grandma
Bemba/Nyanja	Some Zambian dialects
Twatotela	Female Fishing Basket
Insande	Fishing hook
Kalulu	Hare
Tata	Dad

REFERENCES

Brenda Simms (Mrs), Church service sermon, 27 December 2015;

C. S. Nicholls, *Dr David Livingstone,* Sutton Publishing, 1998;

Cecily Mwaniki, *The Wisdom of Ages,* 2014;

Clare Pettit, *Livingstone, I presume?* Harvard University Press, 2007;

Chalwe Bwalya, Story on Reality of how The African Villagers' Hut Tax affected ordinary African (Zambian) families, 2016; Chief Mulala 7 – Interview, April 2012;

Currie A. Marion (Dr), *Livingstone's Hospital,* Author House UK, 2012;

David Livingstone – Wikipedia, the free encyclopedia;

Hugh Macmillan – *Lenshina, Alice Mulenga (1920–1978);*

Keith Katalayi – *Stories of the Zambezi River,* 2016;

Major HDC Dane, *The Geographical Works of Dr Livingstone,* The American Society, 23 April 1874

Papers from Zambian Archives;

Peter Ngelesani Mulutula, Telephone conversations, authenticity and Origins of Ngosa, Kabaso, Shompolo Mulutula, 2015–2016;

Picturing Scotland – *Shetland Islands*, 2014;

Stephen Tomkins, *David Livingstone (The unexplored Story)*, Lion Books, 2013;

Thomas Nelson, *The Holy Bible*, New King James Version 1982;

UN Security Council 1960: Britain's Responsibility in Southern Africa Wikipedia: African Archives' Papers